Reading the Bible in the Age of Francis

Reading the Bible in the Age of Francis

Micah D. Kiel

CASCADE *Books* • Eugene, Oregon

READING THE BIBLE IN THE AGE OF FRANCIS

Copyright © 2019 Micah D. Kiel. All rights reserved. Except for brief quotations in critical publications or reviews, no part of this book may be reproduced in any manner without prior written permission from the publisher. Write: Permissions, Wipf and Stock Publishers, 199 W. 8th Ave., Suite 3, Eugene, OR 97401.

Cascade Books
An Imprint of Wipf and Stock Publishers
199 W. 8th Ave., Suite 3
Eugene, OR 97401

www.wipfandstock.com

PAPERBACK ISBN: 978-1-5326-1745-4
HARDCOVER ISBN: 978-1-4982-4213-4
EBOOK ISBN: 978-1-4982-4212-7

Cataloguing-in-Publication data:

Names: Kiel, Micah D., author.

Title: Reading the Bible in the age of Francis / by Micah D. Kiel.

Description: Eugene, OR: Cascade Books, 2019 | Includes bibliographical references and index.

Identifiers: ISBN 978-1-5326-1745-4 (paperback) | ISBN 978-1-4982-4213-4 (hardcover) | ISBN 978-1-4982-4212-7 (ebook)

Subjects: LCSH: Francis, Pope, 1936– | Bible—Criticism, interpretation, etc. | Catholic Church—Doctrines.

Classification: BS511.3 K4 2019 (print) | BS511.3 (ebook)

Scripture quotations are from New Revised Standard Version Bible, copyright © 1989 National Council of the Churches of Christ in the United States of America. Used by permission. All rights reserved worldwide.

Manufactured in the U.S.A.   06/11/19

Dedicated to my parents, David and Myrna

Contents

Preface | ix
Introduction | xi

1: Francis Reads Scripture | 1
2: Francis's God: A Master of Surprise | 12
3: Francis's Plea: Social Justice for the Poor | 24
4: Francis's Environment: Care for Creation | 42
5: Francis's Blind Spot? Women | 66
6: Francis's Task: Becoming Heralds of Mercy | 82
7: Francis's Disdain: Rigid Adherence to Law | 95
8: Francis's Journey: Uncertainty and Unanswered Questions | 114

Bibliography | 129
Scripture Index | 135

Preface

I NEVER THOUGHT I would publish a first book, let alone a second, and now a third. This one has emerged much more circuitously than my first two. I suppose the book's path, if not linear, at least follows the twists and turns of the Francis papacy. I have worked on this book throughout the last five years in the interstices of my regular life of teaching and university service, family life with lots of travel and baseball, and volunteering at our parish. My students or an interested lay person are the contexts and the audiences I have been thinking of as I wrote this book; I hope it will help such people understand Pope Francis better and learn something about the deep themes of Scripture. The Bible is complex, beautiful, and comes to us from a time and place very different from our own. Its strangeness is part of its power, which I hope to have helped demonstrate.

As always, many thanks are due to my wife, Eleanor, and my children, Harrison and Brendan. St. Ambrose University has also been consistently supportive of my work. Corinne Winter read and commented on a full manuscript and provided helpful insights, for which I am grateful. At many points in this book I refer to "my students." The conversations I have had with students throughout my first eleven years of teaching are a constant source of learning, encouragement, and enjoyment. Though none of them are named, their influence is felt in every chapter and I am very thankful to all of them.

Finally, I dedicate this book to my parents, David and Myrna. When people learn that I converted to Roman Catholicism, the first thing they always ask is "What did your parents think about that?" As Pope Francis has said, our lives are not given to us like an opera libretto, with everything scripted. I am lucky and grateful that my parents have always supported my journey of life and faith, through all its twists and turns.

Introduction

IN THE FALL OF 2013, I sat down with a martini and read the interview of Pope Francis by journalist Antonio Spadaro. This was only a few months after Francis's election. By this point, Francis had already taken the world by storm; he was soon to be named *Time Magazine*'s person of the year. As a Scripture scholar, I could not help putting Francis's words into conversation with various emphases and voices within the Bible. At that point, Francis had made no major publications as pope, and most of the people writing about him were attempting to "read the tea leaves" and predict what Francis might do in the future. This book is different. My goal is to explore within the Bible those things that Francis tends to emphasize, the themes to which he returns again and again. In most cases, the emphases of his ministry have deep scriptural roots, perhaps sometimes more than Francis even realizes. At other times, what we know about Scripture within the world of scholarship might offer some critique of how Francis reads Scripture or what he emphasizes in his ministry.

Since I read the Spadaro interview, the "data" available for examining Pope Francis and the Bible has grown quickly. He has published one full encyclical (*Laudato Si'*) and two major apostolic exhortations (*Evangelii Gaudium* and *Amoris Laetitia*). His morning homilies from St. Martha's guesthouse at the Vatican are published every year and are reported almost daily by various journalists. His airplane press conferences are a treasure trove of witticisms and headline-grabbing statements. While these various forms of communication do not all have the same grounding in Scripture, there are themes that Francis returns to again and again.

INTRODUCTION

The goal of this book is not primarily an exercise in analyzing how Francis reads Scripture, although we will engage in some of that as well. I offer here a brief preview of each chapter.

- In chapter 1, we will begin by analyzing how Francis tends to read the Bible. This will be placed in the context of what he likely learned in his education about Scripture and the different ways that the Roman Catholic Church teaches that Scripture should be read.

- In chapter 2, we explore the idea that God will surprise us. In Scripture, we often find stories that emphasize the idea that God does not follow the expectations of humans. We will see examples of this in 1 Samuel, the Gospel of Mark, and the book of Jonah.

- In chapter 3, we will think about Francis's pervasive call to be with the poor and the marginalized. Perhaps no other hallmark of the Francis ministry has deeper roots in the Bible. We will see the challenging aspects of this in the prophetic book of Amos and in the New Testament in the Gospel of Luke and the book of Revelation.

- Chapter 4 picks up the challenge from Francis's first full encyclical, *Laudato Si'*, which is focused on care for the environment. This encyclical is infused with both scientific and theological information. We will use it as a starting point for exploring the problem of anthropocentrism in the Bible and its unfortunate legacy in environmental destruction. Other texts in the Bible, such as Job, the Psalms, and the Gospel of Mark, offer a different way forward in cultivating a need to care for the environment.

- In chapter 5, we will attempt to answer why Francis so quickly dismisses the idea of women priests. His words are based on church teachings from the last forty years, and the arguments presented are intricately entwined with various biblical texts. We will examine the use of Scripture in the church documents that relate to women and ordained ministry.

- Chapter 6 looks at the Old Testament's wisdom literature and the parable of the good Samaritan in an attempt to further understand Francis's emphasis on mercy. Mercy, for both Francis and the Bible, is one that necessitates concrete action on behalf of the "other."

- In chapter 7, we will look at Francis's opposition to those in the church who long for rigid adherence to law and rules. Parts of the Old and

INTRODUCTION

New Testaments evince a tension between God's graciousness and religious rules; these texts can be instructive still today. We will also consider what we know about the Pharisees historically and whether they are an apt analogy for Francis to use in today's church.

- In the final chapter, we will think about the book of Ecclesiastes, the story of the transfiguration, and Romans 9–11, and coordinate them with how Francis frequently refers to the necessity of openness to unanswered questions. For Francis, there always needs to be an element of uncertainty in faith. There are key scriptural texts that suggest the same thing: we should expect and be open to unanswered questions, and that faith is a journey where the next step is not always clear.

Francis seems to want to be a reformer, to lead the church to think about things in a new way. Because of this, he has met a lot of resistance. The critique may be warranted at times, and we will discuss these instances in the pages that follow. More often, however, I suspect that the resistance to Francis is out of fear or ignorance. Even if Francis does not say so overtly, much of what he says and does is deeply biblical, which I hope to demonstrate in the chapters that follow.

While parts of what I will explore below might be about debates specifically within the Roman Catholic Church, I suspect most of what we explore will appeal broadly to all Christians. Francis is the most prominent face of Christianity for the entire world. The biblical themes of his ministry are incredibly challenging and would require Christians to live in drastically different ways if we were to understand and heed them. I hope that this book will help readers learn something about Pope Francis. But more importantly, I hope readers will learn about those things to which the Bible calls Christians: to act with mercy for all creatures and to be open to a God who wants to push us, both communally and individually, in radical new directions.

1

Francis Reads Scripture

> The study of the sacred Scriptures must be a door opened to every believer.[1]

SCHOLARS LOVE FOOTNOTES, so that is where we begin. I was recently reading a footnote in a book by Richard Hays in which he reflected on the differences among the four Gospels in the New Testament. Hays asks whether Pope Francis might be particularly informed by the Gospel of Luke, which has a unique emphasis on social justice and care for the poor: "Pope Francis, with his emphasis on generosity, peace, and God's love for the poor, embodies a distinctly Lukan sensibility."[2] He then wonders if one could analyze whether Francis's emphases would be reflected in the actual scriptural texts he tended to cite in his writings and public addresses.

Hays's footnote essentially asks the following questions: How does Pope Francis read the Bible? Are there parts of Scripture to which he tends to be drawn? Are there themes he emphasizes? Are there things he avoids? Pope Francis rarely shows his work. He usually does not explain the interpretive strategies on which his work is based. At the same time, we have quite a bit of data that can be analyzed to try to tease out Francis's tendencies when it comes to Scripture. He gives a homily almost every morning in the chapel of St. Martha's Guesthouse, where he lives in the Vatican. Francis has also published one full encyclical and three exhortations, which demonstrate his use of Scripture. Finally, there are writings from before his time as pope that also can give us clues as to how he

---

[1]. Francis, *Evangelii Gaudium*, 175.
[2]. Hays, *Echoes of Scripture*, 440n6.

reads Scripture. In this opening chapter, we will make some observations that emerge from these sources. What we will see is that Francis is a well-trained exegete, one who engages in a wide variety of interpretive methods in his theological and ministerial work.

The Education of Jorge Bergoglio, SJ

Jorge Bergoglio, who would become Pope Francis, first felt called to be a priest in 1953. He started his training at a diocesan seminary, but then applied to be a Jesuit. He found the Jesuit form of community and spirituality appealing. Becoming a full Jesuit would mean years of discernment and education. His overall program would last thirteen years. He took courses in the humanities and received specialized training in philosophy and theology. He also spent time teaching Spanish literature. Through all of this, Bergoglio would have been well-trained in Scripture studies, including ancient languages. He was known for strong ability with Latin.[3] When his philosophical training was over, the school selected the intellectually gifted students for further intellectual pursuits. Jorge Bergoglio was among them.[4]

The backdrop for all of Bergoglio's training was the Second Vatican Council, which lasted from 1962 to 1965. There was, as there still is today, a spectrum of responses to the *aggiornamento*—the updating—that the council wanted to provide. Bergoglio was among those who excitedly embraced the new ideas from the council. He and others worked to publicize its findings at the *Colegio Máximo*, his school in Buenos Aires. He was involved in pasting short texts "mounted on exhibit boards answering questions about what the Council was and what it was setting out to do."[5] Requests poured in for this work to be spread more widely throughout the area.

The impact of Vatican II for Scripture study and for Jorge Bergoglio can hardly be overstated. Austen Ivereigh captures it well: "A new tone was struck, of dialogue and participation, engagement and hope. Catholics would no longer recoil from modernity but would be its midwives, helping to bring to birth a more human world."[6] Such a context for his intellectual training left deep impressions in Francis's ministry as pope and in how he

---

3. Ivereigh, *Great Reformer*, 75.
4. Ivereigh, *Great Reformer*, 76.
5. Ivereigh, *Great Reformer*, 74.
6. Ivereigh, *Great Reformer*, 90.

reads Scripture. Francis consistently presses the idea that Scripture speaks to people and the world today, that it meets us in our own situations, both individually and communally. At the same time, the world is not the thing that holds sway; Scripture speaks prophetically to critique the significant problems in our world—problems of war and violence, poverty and wealth, selfishness and humility.

The way Pope Francis interprets Scripture evinces a combination of his interest in literature with the new guidelines for interpretation from *Dei Verbum*, the document about divine revelation from Vatican II. Francis puts *Dei Verbum* into full deploy, embracing its guidelines for understanding Scripture's historical components. At the same time, Francis has brilliant literary insights into Scripture and finds witty phrases that capture his interpretations in a vivid way.

There are some today who might suggest that Pope Francis is an intellectual lightweight. He does not hail from a well-known doctoral program or theological and philosophical school, like Popes John Paul II and Benedict XVI. Bergoglio actually started a doctoral degree in Germany in the mid-1980s that remains unfinished to this day. What Jorge Bergoglio did have, however, was a broad and strong education that left him with a variety of interests. He also brings to his training a set of unique experiences, including life in a context of colonialism in South America and an exposure to the poor, which he sought out during his education.

What we see, ultimately, from Pope Francis's formation and education is a mix of experiences at important hinge points in the history of Roman Catholicism. His approach is not primarily academic, though informed by academic and historical study of Scripture. His approach is pastoral, although not shy of strong critique. His interpretation often seems improvisational and homespun. But it all demonstrates a deep grounding in his experiences in South America, his strong Jesuit education, and inspiration from the new documents from Vatican II.

The Literal and the Spiritual Senses of Scripture

The Catechism of the Catholic Church outlines different senses of Scripture. Scripture can be read according to the "literal sense" or the "spiritual sense." The "literal sense" means that the interpreter should seek the intention of the original author. God inspires Scripture, but its authors were human and were bound by their own time and place. The job of the interpreter of Scripture's literal sense is to "carefully investigate what meaning the sacred writers really intended and what God wanted to manifest by means of their words."[7] This sets the task for pastors, priests, deacons, and Scripture scholars to understand the writings on their own terms, in accord with the times in which they were written. Interpreters should pay attention to literary forms, the historical circumstances of the authors, and the idioms and situations of the original times and cultures. As we will see, Pope Francis at times engages in this type of interpretation and stresses its importance.

The "spiritual sense" of Scripture is different. Sometimes called the "fuller sense," it can take the interpreter into realms of allegorical or moral interpretations of Scripture. This approach doesn't necessarily ignore the "literal" sense, but it is less concerned with the intention of the original author. It might look for the moral meaning of a given text, or find something to be allegorical. This type of meaning is not constrained by the literal sense of the text or by what the author may have intended. Good spiritual exegesis should not do damage to the original author's aims, but is not bound by them. Let me demonstrate the difference between the literal and the spiritual senses of Scripture by using a specific example.

In the book of Genesis, God sometimes speaks in the plural. For example, in the first creation story in Genesis 1, when God decides to create humanity, the text says: "Let *us* make humankind in *our* image, after *our* likeness" (Gen 1:26; italics added). My students always notice the word "us" and ask: "Is that in the plural because of the Trinity?" The answer to that question is "yes and no." It depends on the sense of Scripture one intends to employ.

If using the literal sense of Scripture, God speaking in the plural cannot be because of the Trinity. The idea of a triune God—Father, Son, and Holy Spirit—is one that develops in the context of early Christianity. This text in Genesis, in the Old Testament or Hebrew Bible, predates the idea of the Trinity by hundreds and hundreds of years. The idea of the Trinity had not yet been revealed or fully grasped, so it cannot be what the writer of Genesis had in mind in his or her own time and place. How, then, does the literal sense of Scripture explain God speaking in the plural? One explanation begins by noting that monotheistic belief did not come to the ancient Israelites at one specific moment in time. Their monotheism emerged slowly, across hundreds of years, in step with their cultural identity. There are many texts in the Hebrew Bible in which the authors presume that the

---

7. Paul VI, "Dei Verbum," 12.

God of the Jewish people is simply a chief God among many others. Psalm 82:1, for example, says: "God has taken his place in the divine council; in the midst of the gods he holds judgment." This text presumes a pantheon of Gods in which Israel's God is prominent. We might call this a vestigial polytheism in the body of the Old Testament, like the appendix in our physical bodies. So, the language in Genesis 1:26 recalls a time when monotheism was not as firmly established as in later time periods. In a literal sense, there is no Trinity here, and it should not be part of the discussion in understanding the perspective of the author in the text's original context.

A "fuller" or "spiritual" sense of Scripture, however, goes beyond the historical context. For Christians reading today, after two thousand years of theological development, we have a robust belief in the Trinity as a unique revelation of God. In this sense, the story in Genesis absolutely testifies to the Trinity. In its fuller sense, the text depicts the inner life of God, an overflowing love for humanity that results in God creating humanity in God's image in the beginning.

Nearly every text in the Bible can be read with these two senses, the literal and the spiritual. The church engages in both types of interpretation partly because of its historical development. For most of the church's history, spiritual exegesis of one type or another was the norm. More recently, with the rise of the modern disciplines of science and history, we have come to understand the important role of the literal sense in our understanding of God's revelation. Both should create in us a sense of humility—God has spoken and yet still speaks. Our interpretations change as humans and the world around us change. The literal and fuller senses of Scripture, when employed properly, allow the church to be sensitive to God's ongoing revelation in continuity with what has happened in the past. Pope Francis himself is fully conversant with these two approaches, and we see him talk about and put into practice each of them at various times.

Francis's Use of the Literal Sense of Scripture

In his apostolic exhortation, *Evangelii Gaudium*, Pope Francis writes about how to interpret Scripture. His words speak specifically to those who will be preachers, but they might be applied to anyone who approaches the Bible. Francis first talks about what should be considered the literal sense of the text, although he does not specifically use that term. He says the interpreter needs to understand the words that are read, taking into account the fact that they are two or three thousand years old. He says that work must be done to understand "what the author primarily wanted to communicate" and the "effect" the author wanted to produce.[8]

At many points in Francis's actual interpretation of Scripture, we see him engage in just this type of work. He rarely "shows his work," but there are hints here and there that Pope Francis is well-trained in the art of exegesis and the literary and historical analysis of Scripture. He is equipped to do the exegetical work to uncover the literal sense of the text, to try to understand historically the intention of the original author. A few examples will demonstrate this fact.

In *Amoris Laetitia*, Francis begins with a long section that focuses primarily on Scripture. Francis quickly turns to the importance of what he calls "fruitful love:"

> The couple that loves and begets life is a true, living icon—not an idol like those of stone or gold prohibited by the Decalogue—capable of revealing God the Creator and Savior. For this reason, fruitful love becomes a symbol of God's inner life . . . This is why the Genesis account, following the "priestly tradition," is interwoven with various genealogical accounts.[9]

Two things here are noteworthy in how Francis is interpreting the book of Genesis. First, he refers to the "priestly tradition." This shows us Francis's training in Scripture studies. Over the last one hundred years, scholars have recognized a variety of different sources that have been incorporated into the final form of the book of Genesis. In other words, Genesis does not really have one author, but is more of an anthology of originally separate sources. This theory, called the documentary hypothesis, lies behind most attempts to understand the literal sense of the text of Genesis. The fact that Pope Francis throws this reference into his analysis tells us that he sees this as a particular emphasis of the priestly source, one of the sources for Genesis.

Second, Francis also offers an explanation for the long genealogies one finds at the beginning of Genesis. Note what answer Francis does not give for these: he does not say, "and these lists of names give us the actual genealogical information of the descent of the Hebrew people." He does not take them as historically reliable pieces of information, but instead provides them a literary interpretation. He essentially asks this question: what

---

8. Francis, *Evangelii Gaudium*, 147.
9. Francis, *Amoris Laetitia*, 11.

function do these lists of names have in their original context for the final author/editor of Genesis? He connects the genealogies with the repeated calls for humanity to be fruitful and multiply. When brought together, these two features of the book of Genesis reinforce each other. What better way to demonstrate a call to be fecund than by giving a bunch of lists of people and their offspring?

In just a couple of sentences at the beginning of *Amoris Laetitia*, Francis has demonstrated his facility with the literal sense of the text. He clearly employs both historical and literary methods of trying to uncover the meaning of the opening chapters of the book of Genesis.

There are many other places where we can get hints of Francis's exegetical training. In *Laudato Si'*, he refers to the Babylonian exile, which provoked a "spiritual crisis" for the Jewish people. He uses this as a backdrop and explanation for a particular emphasis on the role of God as the creator in biblical literature that hails from this time period. In the same chapter, he also discusses the early texts in Genesis, referring to them as "ancient stories, full of symbolism," and that they testify to the interconnectedness of all reality. Here Francis suggests what my students often find shocking: when we analyze the types of literary forms in the book of Genesis, we conclude that these stories are not "historical." They are myth, legend, or some similar type of literature. This is exactly what *Dei Verbum* tells readers of Scripture to do: to understand the Bible in terms of the kind of literature it actually is. Calling the creation texts in Genesis "myths" or "stories" does not undermine their truth. In fact, the opposite is the case. Only by reading a text according to the kind of literature it actually is can one find a proper understanding of its author's intent. By employing these methods, we see Pope Francis following the type of interpretive strategies called for in *Dei Verbum*, the document about revelation that was part of the reforms of Vatican II, released during the formative years of his education.

Finally, Pope Francis brings the same historical and literary tools we've seen him apply to Genesis and uses them on New Testament texts as well. He is honest about the fact that the authors of the New Testament were bound by their own time and place. For example, in *Gaudete et Exsultate*, he says that the "biblical authors had limited conceptual resources" for understanding certain realities. He turns to the example of how epilepsy was misconstrued in the ancient world as demonic possession, but we today know it as a medical condition.[10]

---

10. Francis, *Gaudete et Exsultate*, 160.

Francis also sometimes describes the differences among the four Gospels in the New Testament. For example, also in *Gaudete et Exsultate*, he highlights the differences in the beatitudes in Luke and Matthew (which we will explore in depth in chapter 3 of this book). These two Gospels tell similar versions of the same story, but the differences are significant. In Matthew's Gospel, Jesus says, "Blessed are the poor in spirit" (5:3), whereas in Luke Jesus says "Blessed are you who are poor" (6:20). Francis notes this specific difference and focuses on Luke's version, which highlights physical, not spiritual, poverty. For Francis, this emphasis on real poverty is essential because it then calls Christians to live "a plain and austere life."[11] This may offer a bit of an answer to the query from Richard Hays with which we began this chapter. Francis seems particularly interested in Luke's unique vision.

In the same reflection from *Gaudete et Exsultate*, Francis refers to the Hebrew word, *anawim*, which refers to the meek (see, for example, Psalm 37:11). While this word and concept may or may not be relevant in Matthew and Luke (which were written in Greek), it shows Francis's awareness of the original languages of the Scriptures and the shades of meaning that can be provided by knowing and understanding them. He often refers to the original language in order to get a better grasp on what a text is trying to say. In his homily on 1 Kings 19, he transitions from the "still small voice" in which Elijah discerned God's presence to what the original language conveys, "a resonant whisper of silence."[12]

While the details presented here are anecdotal, indications of Francis's training in the historical and literal sense of Scripture should be clear. He is invested in an accurate reading of the literal sense of the biblical texts. He pays attention to history, literary forms, and ancient languages to help him understand the authors' intentions. This emphasis should not surprise us, as it emerges from his education and training, particularly the era in which he was trained.

Francis's Use of the Spiritual Sense of Scripture

Though Pope Francis is invested and trained in the literal sense of Scripture, he frequently engages in the spiritual or fuller sense of Scripture as well. In his

---

11. Francis, *Gaudete et Exsultate*, 70.
12. Francis, *Morning Homilies III*, 169.

homilies, for example, he often pays no heed to the historical situation or the mind of the author and moves instead to a spiritual interpretation.

Francis uses the spiritual sense in a homily that focused on the genealogy at the very beginning of the Gospel of Matthew (1:1–17). A genealogy seems like a boring way for Matthew to start a book; it's nothing other than a list of names. After pointing out that it is "not a telephone book," Francis finds among the people listed examples of sinfulness and holiness.[13] Noting some of the names who are heroes of the faith, but who also had their dark sides (particularly David and Solomon), Francis points out that they were sinners with whom God also "made history."[14] This interpretation of Matthew's genealogy has deep roots in church history. In the fourth century, Saint Jerome popularized such a reading by suggesting that having sinners among the genealogy was a way of prefiguring Jesus's role as the one who saves from sin. Pope Francis expands his interpretation from just the heroes in the genealogy to include all believers. God is not just the God of Abraham, Isaac, and Jacob, but also "Peter, Marietta, Armony, Marisa, Simon, of everyone. He takes his surname from us. God's surname is each of us."[15] I doubt that this interpretive move from Pope Francis fits what Matthew originally intended. In a fuller sense, however, it testifies that through the incarnation, God insists on being involved intimately with humanity, to share in our humanity. The context for this homily was near the end of advent. Francis capitalized on the imminent feast of Christmas, finding a spiritual reality to which the text testifies. His reading is in continuity with Matthew's intentions, but expands upon them and finds new ways for its meaning to speak today.

Francis occasionally uses full-blown allegory to interpret Scripture. In a homily from March 2015, Pope Francis uses three women in Scripture as allegories of the church. The first woman is Susannah from the book of Daniel. False accusations were made against her, but she remained strong and resolute amidst many calumnies. She represents, for Pope Francis, a holy church that is assailed by outside forces. A second woman, the one caught in adultery in John 8, allegorically represents a sinning church. A final woman, the widow from the parable of the unjust judge in Luke 18, suffers because she is needy. This allegorically represents a needy church. In all three cases, Francis's allegorical interpretation sees a lack of mercy. His allegorical interpretation

---

13. Francis, *Morning Homilies II*, 146.
14. Francis, *Morning Homilies II*, 147.
15. Francis, *Morning Homilies II*, 147.

extends not just to the three women, but also to the men with whom they interact in their respective stories. Susannah was accused unfairly. The woman caught in adultery was assailed by those who rigidly adhere to the law. The poor widow was oppressed by a judge who only cared for himself. Francis summarizes his interpretation this way:

> Corruption did not allow them [the adversarial characters in these three stories] to understand what mercy is, that one must be merciful. The Bible tells us that justice is to be found in mercy. The three women: the saint, the sinner and the needy, allegorical figures that represent the Church, suffer for lack of mercy. And God's people today can find themselves before "judges" who lack mercy, both in a civilian environment and in an ecclesiastical one. Where there is not mercy there is no justice. When God's people come close asking for forgiveness, it often finds itself condemned by one of these judges.[16]

When I first saw the headline for this daily homily from Pope Francis, I was nervous that he would offer a misogynistic allegory, using women in a way that might not uphold their dignity. But when we take the time to understand his allegorical interpretation, he is actually less interested in the role of the women as he is in those who set up barriers to the experience of mercy in the church. In doing so, Francis hits upon what may be the most returned to theme of his entire papacy: the absolute primacy of God's mercy.

As someone who is trained as an exegete within the realm of scholarship, I have a difficult time with the spiritual sense of Scripture. I have been trained to seek the mind of the author, as best as possible, and to give a reading that comports with what we know based on historical plausibility. Spiritual exegesis, however, has been the dominant method of interpretation across the centuries in the church and is still clearly a component of how the Roman Catholic Church says Scripture can and should be read. Thus, we find it a part of the way that Pope Francis approaches the Bible.

Conclusion

This brief chapter has laid out some of the contours of how Pope Francis reads the Bible, particularly as it relates to church teaching about Scripture. The primary aim of this book, however, is not simply to analyze how Francis reads the Bible (although we will do so at times). My goal is

16. "Pope," para. 4.

different: to explore within Scripture those themes that Francis tends to emphasize. As we do this, we will turn to examples that Pope Francis himself seems not to. We will also exclusively use the literal sense of Scripture, an attempt to understand the Bible's authors on their own terms. At many points, this will allow us to continue to analyze how Francis reads, but this book is a broader interpretive and theological enterprise and does not restrict itself only to those interpretations that Pope Francis himself has offered. The themes of Francis's ministry were evident from the very beginning: the poor and marginalized, the environment, mercy and forgiveness, a concern about excessive rigidity regarding rules and the law, and the role of women. These themes, and others, are those to which we will now turn. We will certainly get a sense of what Pope Francis has said about these issues, but at the same time will explore, sometimes in great detail, what Scripture might be saying about them.

2

Francis's God: A Master of Surprise[1]

> God is always a surprise, so you never know where and how you will find him.[2]

MANY YEARS AGO, MY wife threw me a surprise birthday party. I was blindfolded, driven across town, and unloaded into a cavernous room. When the blindfold was removed, I saw a circle of about thirty friends and family. I had no control of the guest list; I didn't pick the menu; I didn't know what was going to happen. I was terrified.

Pope Francis seems to want to drive the church someplace new and rip off the blindfold. This desire is grounded in his understanding of a God who surprises. A surprising God might terrify us because it removes control mechanisms meant to keep us feeling safe. Francis's surprising God is not merely for the sake of innovation; it's not a mechanism for progressiveness. For Francis, a surprising God creates the challenge of obedience. It is easy to obey God if what God calls for falls in line with our habits and competencies. Openness to the future of a surprising God, for Francis, is part of our "heedfulness" to God.[3]

Pope Francis seems fond of the story of Jonah, which he uses as an exhortation not to run away from the Lord's surprise. He wants to make sure that people do not shut the door on God. For Francis, the gospel is constantly new because God is always meeting humanity anew in the midst of our current situations. This God of surprises recurs throughout Scripture. Francis

---

1. See Juel, *Master of Surprise*.
2. Spadaro, "Interview with Pope Francis," para. 81.
3. Francis, *Morning Homilies II*, 177.

himself turns to two specific examples that we will explore in this chapter: a story from the book of 1 Samuel and the book of Jonah, to find a God who surprises. In between these two, we will consider the Gospel of Mark, which attempts to profile God as one who constantly surprises.

1 Samuel 15

The books of 1 and 2 Samuel tell the stories of the early Israelite kingship under Saul, David, and Solomon.[4] One of the central themes in the first half of the book of 1 Samuel is Israel's desire for a king. God does not want them to have a king because that would mean they had rejected God as their king. Nevertheless, God relents and allows them to have a king. The first king is Saul, anointed by the prophet Samuel. His reign is rocky. He makes an oath that endangers his son, Jonathan (1 Sam 14:24–46). He makes a sacrifice against Samuel and God's wishes (1 Sam 13). Saul's ultimate undoing occurs in chapter 15. God tells Saul that he will be God's agent of punishment on the Amalekites and that he should destroy all living things in the process. Saul completes the task, but kept "the best of the sheep and of the cattle and of the fatlings, and the lambs, and all that was valuable, and would not utterly destroy them" (1 Sam 15:9).[5] Saul only destroyed the things that were despised and worthless. In other words, by keeping the best of the animals, Saul did not fully carry out God's instructions.

Immediately, the word of the Lord comes to Samuel, proclaiming: "I regret that I made Saul king, for he has turned back from following me, and has not carried out my commands" (1 Sam 15:10). This leads to a funny exchange. Samuel hunts down Saul to confront him about what he did and to make known God's decree. To paraphrase their conversation:

> Saul: "It's done. I did what God asked."
>
> Samuel: "Then why are my ears filled with the bleating of goats and the mooing of cows?"
>
> Saul: "Um, the people did it."
>
> Samuel: "Just stop right there."

---

4. We ought not to take these stories as straight history; they probably combine various historical legends and stories, all of which have been edited to present a certain theological viewpoint.

5. Unless otherwise noted, all biblical quotations are from the New Revised Standard Version.

Samuel goes on to explain Saul's disobedience:

> "Has the LORD as great delight in burnt offerings and sacrifices,
>   as in obedience to the voice of the LORD?
> Surely, to obey is better than sacrifice,
>   and to heed than the fat of rams. (1 Sam 15:22)

In other words, God says that even faithful religious observance does not remove the need for a more basic type of obedience. After this episode, Saul tried to ask for forgiveness, but it was too late. God had rejected him from being king because Saul had rejected God.

God's order to kill all living things may seem extreme (and it certainly is). However unpalatable, the order emerges from previous stories in the Old Testament. Deuteronomy 20 distinguishes between two types of military victories. For normal cities that God delivers into the hands of the Israelites, they are to kill all the males. In these spoils, the women, children, and livestock may be kept as "booty" (Deut 20:14). For those cities in the land God gave them as an inheritance, they were not to let "anything that breathes remain alive." In other words, for the cities in the promised land, everything was to be destroyed. The Amalekites, however, are a special case. Exodus 17 tells the story of how the Amalekites went out of their way to attack the Israelites as they journeyed out of Egypt. In Exodus 17:14, God promises to have future revenge on the Amalekites, and that they are to "blot out the remembrance" of the Amalekites (Deut 25:19). The Amalekites are not among those cities in the promised land for whom total destruction would have been ordered. Yet God's remembrance of Amalek's attack in Exodus finally comes to fruition in 1 Samuel. Even if Saul or the Israelites had forgotten, God's decree to Saul was clear: "kill both man and woman, child and infant, ox and sheep, camel and donkey" (1 Sam 15:3).

Pope Francis delivered a homily on this text (along with Mark 2) on January 20, 2014. Francis suggests that Saul was following his habits, that God had given him a surprising order that Saul refused to follow. Given what we just explored in Deuteronomy and the background of the Amalekites, however, I suggest that Francis might be misreading this story. Complete annihilation of the Amalekites is exactly what Saul should have expected to be his marching orders. Francis does not seem aware of the textual backdrop about the Amalekites, setting it up as if total destruction would have been a surprise to Saul. Francis nevertheless suggests that

Saul wanted to follow his habits and offer some of it to the Lord and keep some for himself.[6]

More problematic in Francis's interpretation is that God's newness equates with the annihilation of a people: God commands Saul to "utterly destroy all that they have; do not spare them, but kill both man and woman, child and infant, ox and sheep, camel and donkey" (1 Sam 15:3). In Francis's interpretation, God surprises through incalculable violence.

How does Francis come to such a reading of 1 Samuel, looking for a God of surprises? He is likely reading the Old Testament text through the lens of the New Testament. Mark 2:18–22 narrates Jesus's metaphor about not putting new wine into old wineskins. Old wineskins do not have the necessary elasticity for the expansion of fermenting grapes. Jesus suggests that when something new comes along, it can't be poured into what is old. Jesus makes this statement when questioned about why he does not follow some traditional religious practices, particularly fasting. God's new message (new wine) also requires new vessels (new wineskins) that are supple, adaptable, and ready for change. In other words, the God profiled in this story in Mark's Gospel is one of change and surprise. Humans must be ready to adapt to what God will do in the future. God controls the future, not humans.

When discussing this story in Mark's Gospel, Clifton Black suggests that human attempts to control what God will do are doomed to fail. Such attempts are like old wineskins that, when presented with God's movement, are doomed to break and spill wine everywhere. As Black says: the claims of Jesus threaten "those who adopt unsuitable strategies that make only a bigger mess of what they try to fix."[7] Black's words would apply to the story of Saul in 1 Samuel 15 as well. We do not know for certain Saul's intentions: perhaps he disobeyed out of habit, perhaps out of greed, perhaps he just followed the people, as he himself suggested to Samuel. Whatever the motivation, he was calling an audible, changing the script, putting himself in the driver's seat. He tried to pour new wine into an old wineskin, which resulted in a bigger mess and God rejecting him as king. The lack of obedience in Saul's action is idolatry, a refusal to allow God to be God. As Samuel tells him, obedience is better even than sacrifice.

Saul's true sin here was disobedience, a desire to be the one who decides and is in control, rather than God. The lectionary combines this

---

6. Francis, *Morning Homilies II*, 179.
7. Black, *Mark*, 96.

story with Mark, in which Jesus said, "no one puts new wine into old wineskins; otherwise, the wine will burst the skins, and the wine is lost, and so are the skins; but one puts new wine into fresh wineskins" (Mark 2:22). So, while a God of "surprise" might fit Mark's Gospel better than the story in 1 Samuel, Pope Francis reads these two texts together to find a deeper issue. Heeding God's word is more fundamental than anything else, even the trappings of religious practice—in this case, traditions of sacrifice that are usually pleasing to God.

A Surprising God in the Gospel of Mark

If we return to Mark's Gospel, we find that one of its major themes is a God of surprises. The wine and wineskin image from Mark 2 introduced for us the idea of God's newness. The opening line of the Gospel establishes the same—when the word "gospel" rings out in its opening line, the reader is immediately prepared for something new. This word was used in the ancient Roman world to refer to a good report, such as a victorious battle or an important royal birth. The Gospel itself, by its very definition, is new. What the newness looks like, however, and what exactly it means for the characters in Mark's Gospel (and, I would add, for the Gospel's readers today), is one of manifold surprises.

We begin in chapter 4, where Mark's Jesus presents a series of parables. The first, the parable of the sower (4:1–20), seems straightforward enough. A profligate farmer casts seed about. It falls everywhere and only takes lasting root in those places that are good soil. Who exactly Mark understands to be good soil, however, is not immediately clear. We might expect it to be the disciples, those who were "around" Jesus. But they don't understand either: "Do you not understand this parable? Then how will you understand all the parables?" (4:13). The parable of the sower and its explanation (4:1–20) leaves the reader wondering who is, and who is not, the good soil, who is on the inside, and who is on the outside.

Mark compounds these questions with short parables that describe the kingdom of God. In the first (4:26–29), the kingdom of God is like someone who scatters seed and then goes to bed. The seed sprouts and grows all on its own. The one who scattered it is flabbergasted; how it grows, he or she "does not know how" (4:27). The kingdom is also like a mustard seed, something small and overlooked, but once planted, becomes a place of refuge and solace (4:30–32). These parables suggest that the kingdom of God is overlooked, independent, self-sufficient, and potent. It defies expectations and resists human control. It is a complete and utter surprise.

The concluding story in Mark 4 tells of Jesus calming a storm (4:35–41). The disciples are terrified and wake Jesus up. He rebukes the wind and tells the storm to calm down, which it does immediately. Jesus then berates them for their fear and lack of faith: "Why are you afraid? Have you no faith?" (Mark 4:40). Faith and fear, for Mark, are paired opposites. The opposite of faith is not a lack of faith, but fear. Faith for Mark is not a set of propositions to which one intellectually assents. It's not signing on the dotted line agreeing to a creed. Faith, for Mark, is more about fortitude, more about what's in your gut than what is in your head. Our translations often do us a disservice, translating Mark 4:41 and the disciples' response as: "and they were filled with great awe." This translation is very bad. The Greek literally says: "they feared a great fear." The disciples are utterly terrified. Getting this translation correct is important, because Mark seems to pull the rug out from under anyone who wants to hold on to the disciples as paragons of faith and fortitude. Mark leaves his reader at the end of chapter 4 with confirmation that the disciples are not the good soil and wondering who is.

Enter a crazy, screaming, naked man possessed by a demon, dashing himself with rocks. Mark 5 leaves the disciples behind; they are either an afterthought or too afraid to get out of the boat. A demon-possessed man runs up to Jesus and knows exactly who he is, providing a contrast with the disciples' last statement in chapter 4: "Who is this?" The demon-possessed man knows that Jesus is the son of the most-high God (5:7). Jesus sends the demons out of the man and into nearby pigs, who rush into the sea and drown. The news spreads quickly, and people gather to see what had happened. When they see the man, now clothed and in his right mind, they are afraid (5:15).

Several years ago, I was teaching about Mark's Gospel in a small Roman Catholic parish in an Iowa town that time forgot. The Catholic school was shuttered. Cornfields encroached the edges of town. Time encroached on its inhabitants. I was playing my professor role as best I could by wearing jeans and a sport coat and flapping my arms in excitement over the story about the demoniac and the pigs. A man in the back row in overalls (they were all in overalls) raised his hand. He said, "I'm a hog farmer—we're all hog farmers—and I don't know if you know this, but pigs can swim." I didn't know. The industrialized hog farming in Iowa doesn't allow pigs to showcase their aquatic acumen. This farmer was incensed because he thought that the emotional reaction of the townspeople in the story was wrong. They should be mad, he said, not afraid. So far as I can tell, all the Oxford, Harvard, and Princeton PhDs in the world's history had never made this simple observation about Mark's story. It led to a fascinating discussion about the ways in which the story is not realistic. He was right—the people should have been mad that their way of life had been drowned in the lake. This observation, however, only makes Mark's aims all the clearer.

Mark's story suggests that more than their livelihood was at stake in this story. From society's point of view, the demoniac had been dealt with. Their chains were not strong enough to keep him bound, but they had sufficiently ostracized him from society. He was limited to the hillside and the tombs. The problem had been dealt with by exclusion. Then Jesus arrives, liberates the man, and brings him right into the center of town, completely changed. Surprise! They fear because their control was wrested from them. God's kingdom does not unfold in the way they expected—it does not play according to society's rules. It takes root and grows in those most overlooked and insignificant (like a mustard seed). It sprouts up without human cultivation. It does its own thing. It's a total surprise. In Mark's Gospel, the demoniac is the good soil, and when the townspeople realize this, they think, "if he can do this, then what is next?" They fear God's graciousness and the unknown. A God who is free is a God to be feared.

Pope Francis alludes to the parable of the sower when talking about how God is a surprise. He says, "Although the life of a person is a land full of thorns and weeds, there is always a space in which the good seed can grow."[8] This is certainly right, but Mark's Gospel seems to want to push even farther. The stories and parables in chapters 4–5 suggest even more radically that it is the life that seems most thorny, the most problematic, the place with no hope, where God breaks most dramatically into the world, where God's kingdom erupts.

Mark's story of the demoniac adds one more component to an understanding of Francis's theology of God's newness. It is not newness just for its own sake; it is not a cult of innovation or progress. There is content to the newness: God's mercy and graciousness. After the people's fear, they beg Jesus to leave, and he does. As he embarks, the former demoniac asks if he can come along with Jesus. Jesus refuses, telling the man to "go home to your friends, and tell them how much the Lord has done for you, and what mercy he has shown to you" (4:19). The surprise of Jesus here is

---

8. Spadaro, "Interview with Pope Francis," 82.

graciousness and mercy poured out on those who do not deserve it: the recalcitrant, the thorny, the problems. Mercy is the surprise that people don't want because it means they have no way of predicting what God will do and to whom God will do it. As Thomas Merton says, "The mercy of God, unknown and caricatured and blasphemed by some of the most reputable squares, is the central reality out of which all the rest comes and into which all the rest returns."[9]

Jonah's Surprise

We turn for a final biblical exploration of a God of surprises to Jonah, one of the most profound stories in the Bible. This story is imbued with a sense of God's graciousness and humanity's unwillingness to allow it to proceed. As such, it partners thematically with what we discussed already in Mark 4–5.

While most of us might have a Sunday-school familiarity with the story of Jonah, there are details here that often go unreported. The story starts quickly. God tells Jonah to go to Nineveh and to "cry out against it" because "their wickedness has come up before me" (Jonah 1:2). Jonah disobeys and books passage on a ship headed in the opposite direction. The story progresses for two chapters without the reader knowing why Jonah disobeyed. He gets thrown overboard and swallowed by a big fish that God sends his way. Jonah prays a song of thanksgiving for God's help in a time of distress.

After the fish spews Jonah onto the shore, the word of the Lord comes to Jonah again, and this time he obeys. He walks throughout the large city of Nineveh proclaiming that God will overthrow them in forty days. Something amazing happens: the people listen, repent, and God relents from punishing them: "God changed his mind about the calamity that he had said he would bring upon them; and he did not do it" (Jonah 3:10). Finally, we find out that Jonah was angry because he didn't want God to forgive them: "That is why I fled to Tarshish at the beginning; for I knew that you are a gracious God and merciful, slow to anger, and abounding in steadfast love, and ready to relent from punishing" (Jonah 4:2). Jonah rejects the idea of God's mercy and graciousness.

Jonah sat sulking at the edge of the city, and God sent a bush to shade him from the heat of the sun. This made Jonah happy. The next day, God

---

9. Shannon and Bochen, *Life in Letters*, 300.

sent a worm to destroy the bush. This made Jonah angry. In what might be a slight overreaction, Jonah asks God for death: "it is better for me to die than to live." God asks Jonah if it was okay for him to be angry about the bush, and Jonah says, "Yes, angry enough to die." God's response, which closes the book, is worth quoting in full:

> You are concerned about the bush, for which you did not labor and which you did not grow; it came into being in a night and perished in a night. And should I not be concerned about Nineveh, that great city, in which there are more than a hundred and twenty thousand persons who do not know their right hand from their left, and also many animals? (Jon 4:10–11)

The book of Jonah ends with a question, one that is never answered. While the story of Jonah is partly about obedience, at a deeper level it is about control and self-centeredness. Jonah wants to write his own story and to be the one who decides Nineveh's fate. He doesn't think they deserve God's mercy. The surprise for Jonah is not that God is merciful; he knew that all along (it's the reason he fled in the first place). The surprise is that God refuses to let Jonah have control. God has every right to do what God wants.

In a homily on Jonah, Pope Francis suggests that Jonah wanted to be his own author: "Jonah had a plan for his life: he wanted to write his story well."[10] He then turns the question to those listening today: "do we allow God to write our life story or do we want to write it ourselves?"[11] Asking this question, and answering it the way he thinks we should, requires an uncomfortable openness to God's newness. He asks further: "are you able to find God's word in our everyday story, or are you ruled by your own ideas, which don't allow the Lord's surprise to speak to you?"[12] Francis here is calling for obedience. This is not obedience to the way things have always been, but to the way they will be. Only God knows the path. God's newness dangles like the question at the end of Jonah.

Conclusion: From a God of Surprises to a Surprising Pope

The word "surprise" may encapsulate and summarize Francis's papacy as well as any other. His election was a surprise, although insiders knew that

---

10. Francis, *Morning Homilies II*, 53.
11. Francis, *Morning Homilies II*, 54.
12. Francis, *Morning Homilies II*, 54.

FRANCIS'S GOD: A MASTER OF SURPRISE

he was runner-up in the 2005 conclave that elected Cardinal Ratzinger as Pope Benedict XVI. As Francis himself noted, his fellow cardinals went to the ends of the earth to find a bishop for Rome. His actions as pope have been full of surprises. Some of these have been structural. He appointed a council of eight cardinals to advise him on church matters. He relies on his own network of people whom he trusts for essential duties, often cutting out traditional roles for members of the curia.

More widely influential and noticeable, however, are some of the symbolic actions he has taken while pope. While they are not all necessarily groundbreaking, taken in total they evince a pontiff open to God's surprise in his ministry. While in Cuba, for instance, Francis attended a vespers service with various priests and men and women religious. As part of the proceedings, there were presentations by Cardinal Jaime Ortega y Alamina and Sister Yaileny Ponce Torres. After hearing the two of them speak, he decided that his prepared remarks were inappropriate, and he decided instead to interact with what these two people, whom he designated "prophets," had said. He scrapped his planned homily and spoke extemporaneously instead, starting his remarks by saying:

> I had prepared a homily to give now, based on the biblical texts, but when prophets speak—every priest is a prophet, all the baptized are prophets, every consecrated person is a prophet—then we should listen to them. So I'm going to give the [prepared] homily to Cardinal Jaime so that he can get it to you and you can make it known. Later you can meditate on it. And now let's talk a little about what these two prophets said.[13]

This is not necessarily a groundbreaking move by the pope, but it shows a remarkable willingness to be in the moment and to let the spirit lead. Francis does this often, as in his now famous tradition of offering a press conference on his airplane when returning from international journeys.

One more example will demonstrate how Francis seems to implement openness to surprise. In May of 2014, Pope Francis made a trip to Jordan, Israel, and Palestine. Journalist John Allen said that this trip "crystallized Francis's reputation as a pope of surprises" because of the moments that "veered off script and left the pope's advisers scrambling to keep up."[14]

On May 25, Pope Francis was on his way to visit Palestinian president Mahmoud Abbas in Bethlehem and then to celebrate mass in Manger

---

13. *Pope Francis Speaks*, 19.
14. Allen, *Francis Miracle*, 81–82.

Square for the city's Christian population. His route took him past the twenty-six-foot-high barrier that separates Israel from the West Bank, a wall known as the "security fence" in Israel and the "apartheid wall" by Palestinians. With no forewarning, Francis told his driver to stop. He got out of the car and walked to the wall for a five-minute private prayer. Allen describes the pope's spokesman scrambling to find a way to frame this action so that it wouldn't be seen as overly partisan. Palestinians saw it as a sign of solidarity, while in Israel it was seen as a rebuff, angering their foreign ministry experts and prime minister.[15] Whatever the spin, it caught everyone by surprise.

Francis biographer Austen Ivereigh seems to understand the concept of "surprise" as foundational to Francis's ministry as pope. He chooses to end his biography of Francis with this exact concept. Ivereigh claims that, in Francis's ministry, "each day brings novelty,"[16] which he claims is necessary when the Holy Spirit is allowed to act. Pope Francis's penchant for surprise can be tough on those around him. Ivereigh quotes the prefect of the papal household as saying that it can be difficult with the "certain unpredictability in his actions."[17]

For Francis, the fact that God surprises has profound implications for the church. The church should reflect that openness to newness in the future. Ivereigh records Francis's address to thousands in St. Peter's Square in 2014: "If the church is alive, it must always surprise," he said. Ivereigh notes that the pope was grinning mischievously when he said this. I am skeptical of whether or not Ivereigh can discern the mindset behind Francis's grin. Nevertheless, there is no doubt that a God and a church that surprises will keep everyone on their toes: "A Church that doesn't have the capacity to surprise is a weak, sickened and dying Church. It should be taken to the recovery room at once."[18]

It is difficult to avoid reading subtext into Francis's language about surprises. Many recoil at such an idea, especially if it means that Roman Catholics are to disregard previous church teachings because of a new, surprising God. Fr. John Hunwicke, for example, wrote an article suggesting that the job of the pope is not to say "yes" to new things, but to say "no." He suggests that what Francis is doing is appealing to a sense of

---

15. As recounted in Allen, *Francis Miracle*, 81–82.
16. Ivereigh, *Great Reformer*, 396.
17. Ivereigh, *Great Reformer*, 396.
18. Ivereigh, *Great Reformer*, 396.

the Holy Spirit's newness as a "piece of cheap machinery" used to "evade perceived inconveniences in inherited Christian teaching."[19] Hunwicke goes so far as to refer to "his God of Surprises." This is a not-so-subtle suggestion that Francis follows some God other than the true God. While I find this language alarmingly schismatic, there is a legitimate critique here, depending on how new and surprising Francis's proposed actions or changes end up being. Does Francis like a God of surprises simply to justify the changes he wants to make?

What we have seen in this chapter suggests that Francis's God of surprises is not just one of convenience. It is not just a "piece of cheap machinery" used to further his agenda. Francis's theological formulations have deep scriptural roots in both the Old and New Testaments. The same dynamics we saw in Scripture continue today: there is resistance to and fear of God's newness. A surprising God removes mechanisms of human control, which is sure to lead to fear and backlash. The God in the Bible is a God of surprises. Francis seems to be saying that if that gets lost, the church loses its life at the same time.

This chapter began with a quotation from Pope Francis from the beginning months of his time as pope. He claimed that God is always a surprise. Francis has not backed off from this assertion. In his exhortation *Gaudete et Exsultate*, he doubles down on this idea, claiming that "God infinitely transcends us; he is full of surprises." A God who surprises is one that Francis returns to again and again. One might say it is the theological bedrock of how he understands God, humanity, and the world. It is a conception of God that modern Christians should find very challenging, for it forces us not to rest only on the past, but to be open constantly to God's new movement in the future, both in our own lives and within the church. This way of thinking about God could be exhilarating. It may also terrify us, because we didn't create the guest list, and when the blindfold is ripped off, who knows what will be staring back at us? Francis makes this call passionately and beautifully, as he prods the church to move in new ways:

> God is eternal newness. He impels us constantly to set out anew, to pass beyond what is familiar, to the fringes and beyond. He takes us to where humanity is most wounded, where men and women, beneath the appearance of a shallow conformity, continue to see an answer to the question of life's meaning.[20]

19. Hunwicke, "Peter Says No," para. 31.
20. Francis, *Gaudete et Exsultate*, 135.

3

Francis's Plea: Social Justice for the Poor

There is an inseparable bond between our faith and the poor.[1]

The devil always comes in "through the pocket."[2]

IN OCTOBER 2013, FORMER *Fox News* commentator Bill O'Reilly was touting his new book, *Killing Jesus*. He took offence at some of its reviewers, many of whom suggested that he did not take seriously the political and economic components of Jesus's message and how they relate to his death. He invited one of these critics, Dr. Candida Moss, on his show. Although Bill can bluster his way through anything, it was clear that Bill was out of his intellectual league. O'Reilly maintained that Jesus "being for the poor" is a historical fact about the life of Jesus, but that the "giving away your possessions business" is a theological thing, not historical. When Moss confronted O'Reilly with a simple story, such as the one in Luke 18:18–30 in which Jesus tells a rich ruler that he must sell all of his possessions and give them to the poor, O'Reilly's response is telling: "No, that's not true, it's absolutely false. It's a misreading of the gospels."

On the facts, O'Reilly is (not surprisingly) dead wrong. The story about the rich ruler is in all three Synoptic Gospels. I cannot fathom how he can claim it is "not true" with a straight face. On the other hand, his emotional reaction is appropriate and understandable. If we truly understand the economic aspects of Jesus's message and its roots in the Jewish Scriptures, we ought to be incredulous. There is a bumper sticker that I like:

---

1. Francis, *Evangelii Gaudium*, 48.
2. Glatz, "Devil Prefers Comfy, Business-Savvy Church."

"if you're not appalled, you're not paying attention." O'Reilly's incredulity means that he is at least paying attention. If Jesus's words about how we deal with money are taken seriously as a criterion for judgment and eternal life, then, as O'Reilly says, a lot of people are going to hell.

In his inaugural homily, Pope Francis said that he wanted a "poor Church for the poor" and that we will be judged by how we act on behalf of the "hungry, the thirsty, the stranger, the naked, the sick and those in prison."[3] He demonstrated this two weeks later when, on Holy Thursday, he visited a prison in Rome called Casal del Marmo. He washed the feet of twelve people, including women and non-Christians. (He had done something very similar when he became archbishop in Buenos Aires.[4])

Pope Francis's understanding of economic issues emerges from the roots of his own family. His grandparents emigrated from Italy to Argentina in search of better economic opportunity.[5] He had extensive experiences with the poor slums in Buenos Aires, both as a priest and bishop. Austin Ivereigh quotes a priest from Buenos Aires as saying that Bergoglio's visits to the *villas* (slums) was how he "filled his lungs with the oxygen he needed to guide the Church."[6] From the beginning of his ministry, long before he became pope, Francis lived a life focused on the poor.

The church in Latin America in which Francis was formed has been a vanguard in emphasizing the "preferential option for the poor," which means God has a special disposition toward the poor. At times, such emphases came under ecclesiastical suspicion, especially when they were aligned with Marxism. By the time Bergoglio became a cardinal, however, these ties had weakened and were less of a concern. Many of the contours of Francis's understanding of the importance of the poor can be traced to a meeting of the Latin American Episcopal Council (CELAM) at Aparecida, Brazil in 2007. The council referred to those people who are *sobrantes* (the leftovers); a *cultura del descarte* (throwaway culture); and those who are on *las periferias existenciales* (the existential margins). These words and metaphors for talking about the poorest in the world have come to be the bedrock of Francis's papacy.[7]

---

3. As quoted in Allen, *Francis Miracle*, 137.
4. Ivereigh, *Great Reformer*, 241.
5. Ivereigh, *Great Reformer*, 3–5.
6. Ivereigh, *Great Reformer*, 233.
7. All from Ivereigh, *Great Reformer*, 298. Francis's role in the CELAM in 2007 gave him increasing prominence. The council's results were also given a strong stamp of

The Bible consistently emphasizes the important place of the poor in the purview of God. The ancient Israelites had laws that made specific provisions for the orphan, the widow, the poor, and the alien. The prophets in the Old Testament repeatedly call for social justice and for political policy that makes provision for the poor. In the New Testament, language about the poor and the outcast is prevalent in Jesus's words and one of the main organizing principles of his entire ministry. The apostle Paul takes up a collection for the poor in Jerusalem. The book of Revelation critiques a Roman economy of exclusion and obscene luxury. Care for the poor is one of the most pervasive themes in the Bible. Here we will choose three texts to help demonstrate how and why the Bible discusses these issues so pervasively. First, we will discuss the prophet Amos, before turning to two texts from the New Testament: the Gospel of Luke and the book of Revelation.

The Bible not only advocates for the poor and the marginalized, but does so by engaging the political situations of its various time periods. Talking about the poor and possessions is not simply a "theological" category devoid of politics. The Bible offers radical challenges to the economic status quo; such challenges will always be political.

Amos

Introduction to Amos

Amos lived in the middle of the eighth century BCE. At this time, the Hebrew people were divided into two kingdoms: the south (Judah) and the north (Israel). Amos was from the south, living as a shepherd from a town called Tekoa about ten kilometers from Jerusalem. God's message came to him, telling him to prophesy in the northern kingdom. This situates him as an outsider, someone without a background as a prophet, who can speak truth to power.

While it is impossible to reconstruct the historical situation of Amos's day with precision, there are some trends that help form a backdrop for what Amos says. The first half of the eighth century BCE was one of general ascendancy for Israel. Many of the superpowers in their part of the world were not particularly strong at this point in time. As a result, it was a period of territorial and economic expansion in Israel. The evidence suggests that religious activity in the northern kingdom during

---

approval by Pope Benedict XVI.

Amos's day was "thriving."[8] It was a period of relative stability, with a long reign for King Jeroboam. Amos is sent to a situation in which, historically speaking, all seems well: territory is gained, politics are stable, and many people are prospering. The radical message from Amos is that none of that matters if something more basic is not attended to: the care for the poorest of the land. Rather than religious practice, Amos targets "crimes against humanity."[9] Rather than a view from above, Amos provides a view from ground level. Though archeology tells us that everything was going well, the evidence from Amos suggests otherwise: the poor were not equal beneficiaries of society's success.

Social Justice in Amos's Oracles

The book of Amos opens with a series of oracles against the nations that surround Israel: Damascus, Gaza, Tyre, Edom, Ammon, Moab, and Judah. Such an opening may have whipped Amos's audience into a frenzied excitement at God's judgment coming to the nations who surround them. Israel, however, does not escape the judgment:

> Thus says the LORD:
> For three transgressions of Israel,
>   and for four, I will not revoke the punishment;
> because they sell the righteous for silver,
>   and the needy for a pair of sandals—
> they who trample the head of the poor into the dust of the earth
>   and push the afflicted out of the way. (Amos 2:6–7)

The oracle against Israel immediately focuses on economic issues and treatment of the poor. They exchange the righteous for silver and the needy for a pair of sandals.

Amos's language here is vague. He may be alluding to selling people into slavery, especially those who had suddenly become poor. The language could also suggest a predatory loan system or the seizure of family lands (as is the case in Mic 2:1–2 and Isa 5:8).[10] Whatever the specific historical background, it is clear that the "prime sin of Israel is the abuse and oppression of the poor. It is in the domestic scene, not on the international stage, that Israel's crimes

---

8. Andersen and Freedman, *Amos*, 20.
9. Andersen and Freedman, *Amos*, 20.
10. Andersen and Freedman, *Amos*, 310–13. See also Ellis, "Amos Economics," 467–68.

are exposed."[11] The leadership was supposed to be a source of justice, but they are not taking initiative on behalf of the most vulnerable.

Similar economic critiques return throughout Amos. Chapter 6, for example, proclaims "alas" to those who are filled with indulgences and niceties:

> Alas for those who are at ease in Zion,
>   and for those who feel secure on Mount Samaria . . .
> Alas for those who lie on beds of ivory,
>   and lounge on their couches,
> and eat lambs from the flock,
>   and calves from the stall;
> who sing idle songs to the sound of the harp
>   and like David improvise on instruments of music;
> who drink wine from bowls,
>   And anoint themselves with the finest oils.
> Therefore they shall now be the first to go into exile,
>   and the revelry [*marzeaḥ*] of the loungers shall pass away.
> (Amos 6:1, 4–7)

Earlier in Amos, the elites were critiqued for building houses of hewn stone (5:11), a sure sign of affluence in the eighth century BCE. Here, Amos takes us inside those mansions, where the rich eat veal, pluck out songs, and lounge on luxurious beds. The meal named in verse 7 as a *marzeaḥ* is well-known in ancient sources from Amos's day. Many of the actions listed in these verses show up in a variety of literary texts and artistic representations of revelry in Amos's ancient context. This evidence "testifies to the debauchery and incredible expense" in such meals.[12] These words of woe in Amos are attacking luxury, comfort, and idleness. The language suggests that "those in power benefit directly from the oppression" of the poor.[13]

We have now seen Amos's critique of very specific predatory economic practice and obscene luxury in the eighth century BCE. What is his proposed response? Behold the lion:

> Alas for you who desire the day of the LORD!
>   Why do you want the day of the LORD?
> It is darkness, not light;
>   as if someone fled from a lion, and was met by a bear;

---

11. Andersen and Freedman, *Amos*, 308.
12. Carroll, *Contexts for Amos*, 259.
13. Carroll, *Contexts for Amos*, 259.

> or went into the house and rested a hand against the wall,
>> and was bitten by a snake.
> Is not the day of the LORD darkness, not light,
>> and gloom with no brightness in it? (Amos 5:18–20)

God's judgment is coming and no one can escape, like running from a lion and getting mauled by a bear. People will be blindsided. Amos takes well-known biblical ideas—the importance of the day of the LORD and the metaphors of God as light or a lion—and turns them both on their heads. The day of the LORD will be a bad thing, when God will require recompense for injustice. This day that God brings is not light but darkness. It's dire and negative. Amos continues, getting more specific:

> I hate, I despise your festivals,
>> and I take no delight in your solemn assemblies.
> Even though you offer me your burnt offerings and
> grain offerings,
>> I will not accept them;
> and the offerings of well-being of your fatted animals
>> I will not look upon.
> Take away from me the noise of your songs;
>> I will not listen to the melody of your harps. (Amos 5:21–23)

Here, Amos makes it clear that God's primary concern is not with proper worship. As we already noted, the evidence suggests that there was an abundance of proper worship of God during this time period. The songs, sacrifices, and offerings were all being observed properly. According to Amos, God wants something more fundamental. Society and its religious components must be properly aligned with care for the poor. Amos proclaims God's ultimate desire: "But let justice roll down like waters, and righteousness like an ever-flowing stream" (5:24). Amos calls for a deluge of justice.

Amos's words could translate quite directly to our world today. Hordes of people attend church and read their Bible, yet never care for the poor. The accumulation of wealth among the rich continues to expand. 45 percent of the planet's wealth is held by only 0.7 percent of its population.[14] The poor are being left behind today, too. Scholars are usually quick to point out that Amos has no knowledge of modern capitalism, and that he does not condemn "accumulation of wealth *per se*."[15] This may be accurate. Pope

---

14. Statistics from https://inequality.org/facts/global-inequality/. See also Milanovic, *Global Inequality*, 10–45.

15. Ellis, "Amos Economics," 472.

Francis, however, has no qualms about joining his prophetic voice with Amos on this issue. He is quick to point out that the promises of capitalism, while they may have been good for many, have left some out. The poor are permanently excluded from this system; they are the leftovers. This image turns those in persistent poverty into food we couldn't finish and scraped off our plates into the garbage. Francis claims that our modern economic system, which is based on the idea that it will pull people out of poverty, "has never been confirmed by the facts." It expresses, he claims, a "crude and naïve trust in the goodness of those wielding economic power and in the sacralized workings of the prevailing economic system." While all this has been going on, "the excluded are still waiting."[16]

The Gospel of Luke

Each of the four Gospel authors provides a unique spin on who Jesus was. The Gospels are less historical documents than they are icons—artistic representations attempting to grasp the truth of God and Jesus. The author of the Gospel of Luke intends to emphasize God's interest in economic issues, focused on the poor, the outcast, and the lowly. This theme arises at the very beginning of his Gospel, when he chooses shepherds as the group to whom the angels announce the good news of Jesus's birth. Mary's song in response to her pregnancy recapitulates the same note. Starting with herself as an example, Mary broadens the horizon of God's activity to the economic and political realm:

> He has brought down the powerful from their thrones,
>   and lifted up the lowly;
> he has filled the hungry with good things,
>   and sent the rich away empty. (Luke 1:52–53)

Later Luke tells a story about the rich man and Lazarus (16:19–31). Throughout his life, the rich man failed to pay attention to Lazarus, who would sit and beg while dogs licked his sores. All the while, the rich man would feast sumptuously (16:19). Their fates diverge after they die—Lazarus goes to a good place, and the rich man ends up tormented in Hades. A chasm separates them. The rich man, distraught over his fate, begs for a drop of water to cool his tongue, but Abraham responds that he received his reward during his life on earth. Then the man begs that Lazarus be sent to his five rich brothers

---

16. Francis, *Evangelii Gaudium*, 54.

to warn them about their impending fate. The response is stark: "they have Moses and the prophets; they should listen to them" (16:29). Luke draws a parallel between his own emphases and the prophets like Amos: God's fundamental interest in the poor and the outcast.

The best way to get a sense of Luke's interest in the poor is with his version of the beatitudes. Most Christians are very familiar with the Sermon on the Mount from Matthew's Gospel, in which Jesus announces a series of blessings. What many do not know is that Luke has his own version of these Beatitudes. Their subtle differences result in a drastic difference in meaning:

Matthew 5:1–9	Luke 6:17–21; 24–25
When Jesus saw the crowds, he went up the mountain; and after he sat down, his disciples came to him. Then he began to speak, and taught them, saying: "Blessed are the poor in spirit, for theirs is the kingdom of heaven. "Blessed are those who mourn, for they will be comforted. "Blessed are the meek, for they will inherit the earth. "Blessed are those who hunger and thirst for righteousness, for they will be filled. "Blessed are the merciful, for they will receive mercy. "Blessed are the pure in heart, for they will see God. "Blessed are the peacemakers, for they will be called children of God."	He came down with them and stood on a level place, with a great crowd of his disciples and a great multitude of people from all Judea, Jerusalem, and the coast of Tyre and Sidon. They had come to hear him and to be healed of their diseases; and those who were troubled with unclean spirits were cured. And all in the crowd were trying to touch him, for power came out from him and healed all of them. Then he looked up at his disciples and said: "Blessed are you who are poor, for yours in the kingdom of God. "Blessed are you who are hungry now, for you will be filled. "Blessed are you who weep now, for you will laugh . . . "But woe to you who are rich, for you have received your consolation. "Woe to you who are full now, for you will be hungry. "Woe to you who are laughing now, for you will mourn and weep."

There are four observations we need to make as we compare Matthew and Luke's Beatitudes.

First, we must note that these are different versions of the same story. This raises a whole host of historical questions that we will not concern ourselves with. The aim of the Gospel authors was never primarily historical. They were not eyewitnesses to the events (see Luke 1:1–4). Jesus clearly made some sort of speech with blessings in it, but what exactly those blessings looked like when Jesus actually uttered them is a question we cannot answer, primarily because that is not the question Matthew and Luke aim to answer.

Second, the differences in the way these two speeches of Jesus are framed indicate the authors' aims. Matthew has Jesus ascend a mountain and speak only to his disciples. This fits Matthew's overall agenda of presenting Jesus as a new Moses. Jesus, like Moses, goes up a mountain to receive the law. The setting in Luke is the exact opposite. Jesus comes down off a mountain and stands on level ground. We call Luke's version the "Sermon on the Plain." Not only does Jesus descend to a level place, but a multitude surrounds him. Jesus enters the chaos of the people who clamor for a touch or a cure. Luke insists that Jesus seeks out an encounter; he does not separate himself.

Third, the blessings in these two stories are so similar that you might miss the differences unless you read them closely. The first thing to notice is that the grammar is different. In Matthew, the blessings are in the third person, addressed to "they." Luke's Jesus says them in the second person: blessed are "you." This lends immediacy to Luke's message; Jesus is speaking directly to that crowd that is pressing in on him. More shocking than the grammar, however, is the difference in content of the blessings. While Matthew says, "blessed are the poor in spirit," Luke says, "blessed are you who are poor." Matthew says "blessed are those who hunger and thirst for righteousness," while Luke says, "blessed are you who are hungry now." The difference here should not be too hard to discern. Anyone can be poor in spirit; not everyone is poor. I am poor in spirit when my kids are sick or a family member dies, but I am still not poor. Anyone can hunger and thirst for righteousness, but not everyone lacks food. We might describe Matthew's blessings as "spiritualized," while Luke's are focused on real, physical situations.

Finally, Luke's version of this sermon contains an entire section of woes that Matthew's does not.[17] If there was any doubt about Luke's attitude about economic issues, his woes remove it. Jesus pronounces woe on the rich, the full, and those who laugh. The Jesus in Luke's Gospel sees divine activity and judgment through a socioeconomic lens.

---

17. Matthew does have woes, but they come toward the end of his Gospel and are focused mostly on the Pharisees (Matt 23:13–36).

It is not hard to guess why Matthew's Beatitudes are found in church songs and on bulletin covers. We can all find ourselves in Matthew's Beatitudes at different points in our lives. Their breadth gives them their power and tenacity in the tradition. We ought to be careful, however, not to let them overpower Luke's version. Luke's Beatitudes offer a very different vision, one in which many people in American churches have no ability to find themselves. If you have enough money to buy this book, you are probably not among the global poor.

Once my students comprehend the vision of Luke's Jesus, they almost always have the same initial reaction: "But that's not fair!" We tend to structure our religious judgments by prayer or church attendance, or we emphasize having the right position on social and moral issues, such as abortion and gay marriage. Luke's Gospel calls for an adjustment of thinking, one where God's primary aim is to care for the poor. Judgment will come along socioeconomic lines, not those that belong to "religious" or "moral" categories as we have come to understand them.

Another reaction to Luke's emphasis on social justice from my students usually sounds like this: "If we give all our money to the poor, then they'll be rich and we'll be poor. It doesn't solve the problem." This technically might be correct. What Luke proposes is absurd and contains little practical advice. Part of the problem here is a fundamental misunderstanding of what Scripture tries to do. We often read it for instructions on how to live. When I was a kid, I remember my youth pastor comparing the Bible to a road map for our lives. Sometimes this is true, but more often Scripture simply tries to describe God. Who is God? What is God like? What does God care about? Mary's song after the annunciation says nothing about what humans should or should not do. Her song simply describes what God cares about and what God will do. The same is true in Luke 6. Luke is not offering a self-help book on how to get to heaven. He is describing God. The problem arises when we realize that the God Luke describes is one who judges along socioeconomic lines. If Luke is right, then many of us are not going to heaven because of monetary matters. As Jesus says later in Luke's Gospel, "You cannot serve God and money" (Luke 16:13; author's translation).

Luke's Gospel does not offer a specific social program to end poverty, but instead describes where God's attention lies within the human sphere. Here, Pope Francis is very instructive. His insistence that we meet Jesus among the poor and the outcast is exactly what Luke is trying to say. It is not a way of solving the problem, but a way of understanding God. We meet and understand God in the poor. It may well be that some change of action could flow from that encounter, but without the encounter, we miss the point. We can't take Luke's Gospel and craft an economic system based on it. First we must sleep with Luke's shepherds, sit with the sore-ridden Lazarus, and listen to the women who were following Jesus.

Economic Lust: The Book of Revelation

One might be surprised to move to the book of Revelation for an understanding of economic issues in Scripture. What does the apocalyptic culmination of the Bible have to do with how people spend their money? It turns out that Revelation may be the most radical economic book in the entire Bible. It shares the concerns of Amos and Luke, but takes them a step farther. It suggests that any participation in an economy of exclusion and luxury is like aligning yourself with the devil. The economy at the time this book was written was run by the Roman Empire. According to the author of Revelation, the economic system of Rome has become so infected by evil that there is nothing worth saving—God is going to come and blow it all up.

Introduction to Revelation

The book of Revelation scares people, but not for the reasons they think it should. Most people assume that the book was written to predict the future. Nothing could be further from the truth. Revelation is an apocalypse, a type of ancient literature that provided hope and consolation for a suffering community. While it does seem to say a lot about the future, its visions were meant to console the suffering community to which it was written. Revelation offers a clash between God's kingdom and the kingdom of the world. While it may appear as if the forces of evil are in control (in this case, the Roman Empire), God will come very soon and put an end to it all and create a new and better future for the righteous people. Revelation 11:15 reads almost like a thesis statement for the whole book. After blowing the seventh trumpet, loud voices in heaven proclaim: "'the kingdom of the world has become the kingdom of our Lord and of his Messiah, and he will reign for ever and ever.'" Because we live in the context of modern democracies, the political component of such a statement might slip past us. Proclaiming the end of a kingdom suggests that the politics of the age are opposed to the aims of God. God will not stand idly by. Therefore, Revelation is one of the most political books in the Bible. As we will see, one of Revelation's primary complaints about the political situation in ancient Rome was its economy of exclusion and extreme luxury for those few at the top.

Letters to Seven Churches

At the beginning of Revelation, after some introduction and an opening vision, the author of Revelation (named John in the text) writes letters to seven churches at the behest of an angel. These letters give us some insight into the social situation of those who comprised John's community. They were likely facing questions of capitulation to idols and food sacrificed to them within the realm of Greco-Roman polytheism (see 2:14, 20). Moreover, some people were suffering and dying for their faith (e.g., 2:13). In these letters we also find language about wealth and poverty. To the church in Smyrna, John writes that he knows of their poverty, even though they are rich. This suggests a spiritual richness that results from them being materially poor. John says the opposite to the church in Laodicea. They were bragging about their wealth: "For you say, 'I am rich, I have prospered, and I need nothing.' You do not realize that you are wretched, pitiable, poor, blind, and naked" (3:17). John calls for them to "repent" (3:19). From the beginning of the book, then, economics seem to be one of the ethical standards against which John is judging people's actions.

The Beast and Economics

If we jump ahead to Revelation 13, the economic message of the apocalypse comes into sharper focus. Chapter 13 describes two beasts, part of an extended vision that begins in chapter 12. A dragon tries to create havoc in heaven, but fails. As a result, he takes up his stand on the earth. First, a great beast rises out of the sea (13:1). Then another beast rises from the earth (13:11). All of the authority on earth is given to this second beast as it forces all of the earth to worship the first beast. John's original audience would have known that these beasts were veiled references to Rome's emperors.[18] Furthermore, these beasts are connected with the devil, or Satan.

18. At the end of chapter 13, the number 666 is said to represent a person. Using an ancient form of numerology called gematria, the number 666 is an encoded reference to Nero, a notoriously nasty emperor of Rome, known for his murder of Christians. See

The dragon that begins this vision is named as both in 12:9 and the beasts' authority is derived directly from this dragon. The authority of Rome, according to John, comes straight from the devil.

This might leave you asking this question: what about Rome was so bad? What makes this empire satanic, or of the devil? The answer given in chapter 13 (and quite consistently throughout Revelation) is economics:

> Also it [i.e., the beast] causes all, both small and great, both rich and poor, both free and slave, to be marked on the right hand or the forehead, so that no one can buy or sell who does not have the mark, that is the name of the beast or the number of its name. (Rev 13:16–17)

This text has proved generative for all sorts of predictions of the future. When I was young, I was told that someday we would all have computer chips implanted in our wrists in order to purchase food. (This may still come true.) Such predictions are beside the point. John is describing his own context and suggests that any capitulation or participation in the economy of Rome is like aligning oneself with the beast, or Satan. The problem is with Rome's economy. His challenge for those who confess Jesus as the Messiah is to realize that no participation is allowed. There is no gray area. Any participation is like sleeping with a prostitute (see 2:19–23; 17:1–18).[19] Despite this unfortunately misogynistic image, it conveys the idea that there is no room here for compromise. As Brian Blount summarizes:

> John fears that his people will destroy their relationship with Christ by accommodating themselves, through either social fear or economic lust, to a prostituting relationship with Rome.[20]

Schadenfreude—John's Joy at the Downfall of the Rich and Powerful

The phrase "economic lust" provides a good transition to Revelation 18. Here, John writes a lament over the fall of Babylon (which is to be understood as Rome itself). It starts from the perspective of John and his

---

Blount, *Revelation*, 261–63.

19. One significant problem with interpreting the book of Revelation is its misogyny. Other than the woman clothed with the sun in chapter 12, women are either prostitutes or brides. There are many good scholarly treatments of this topic. See especially Pippin, *Death and Desire*, and Rossing, *Choice Between Two Cities*.

20. Blount, *Revelation*, 309.

community, coming from the voice of an angel who proclaims Rome's downfall and calls for people to come out from her and to avoid her sins (18:4). The speech then turns into a lament from the perspective of those who have tied their fortunes to Rome. The kings of the earth, the merchants, and those with a financial stake in the empire all lament over what they will lose. Here it is worth quoting Revelation at length:

> And the merchants of the earth weep and mourn for her, since no one buys their cargo any more, cargo of gold, silver, jewels and pearls, fine linen, purple, silk and scarlet, all kinds of scented wood, all articles of ivory, all articles of costly wood, bronze, iron, and marble, cinnamon, spice, incense, myrrh, frankincense, wine, olive oil, choice flour and wheat, cattle and sheep, horses and chariots, slaves—and human lives.
> The fruit for which your soul longed
> has gone from you,
>   and all your dainties and your splendor
>   are lost to you,
>   never to be found again!
> The merchants of these wares, who gained wealth from her, will stand far off, in fear of her torment, weeping and mourning aloud,
>   "Alas, alas, the great city,
>   clothed in fine linen,
>   in purple and scarlet
>   adorned with gold,
>   with jewels, and with pearls!
>   For in one hour all this wealth has been laid waste!"
> And all shipmasters and seafarers, sailors and all whose trade is on the sea, stood far off and cried out as they saw the smoke of her burning,
>   "What city was like the great city?"
> And they threw dust on their heads, as they wept and mourned, crying out,
>   "Alas, alas, the great city,
>   where all who had ships at sea
>   grew rich by her wealth!
>   For in one hour she has been laid waste." (18:11–17)

Here we can see John's *Schadenfreude*, a German word that means "joy at the misfortune of others." John asks his community to think of Rome's downfall from the perspective of the rich and the powerful, who cry over the city because their fortunes will be lost. The list of goods mentioned, including spices, cloth, types of wood, and even humans, are an accurate list of the luxury goods enjoyed by the elites of Rome.[21] The goods listed demonstrate Rome's "addiction to consumption" that came at the "expense of the peoples of the empire."[22]

When we see chapters 13 and 18 side by side, we get a deeper look into John's critique of his economic context. Those lamenting Rome's downfall in chapter 18 are not wringing their hands over the choices they've made. Nor does John suggest in chapter 13 that the problem stems from the accumulation of people's bad choices. The problem with the ancient economy is structural. Evil has been bred into the very heart of the system. That is why John permits no participation in it whatsoever. Seeing the problem as structural also helps explain John's response. The only way to deal with a structural problem is to blow up the structure. John does not propose a new policy, a new form of charity, or a social program to help the poor. The world is so infected that annihilation is the only solution. John looks out at the world and sees a situation where the rich get richer and the poor are increasingly left out and overlooked. He responds with a revelation that God's destruction of Rome is imminent.

The "Economy" of the New Jerusalem

We turn, finally, to the end of the book of Revelation. Chapters 21 and 22 describe God creating a new heaven and a new earth after the old had passed away. A new Jerusalem descends to the new earth, built with an array of precious jewels, stones, and other valuable items.

In this new creation, "the sea was no more," a startling lack of continuity with our planet as we know it. John's omission of the sea makes sense in light of his economic critique of the Roman Empire. The sea was the seat of Rome's power, the primary engine for trade. It is how most of Rome's luxury goods (like those listed in chapter 18) were transported. Removing the sea undercuts the basis of their economic system. It would be like envisioning our economics today without a highway system or without Wall Street.

The final chapter of Revelation focuses on life within this new Jerusalem. One river flows through the city, and on its banks grows the tree of life. It produces different fruit each month of the year and its leaves are for the healing of the nations. This vision constitutes an economic alternative to what Rome offered: one river and one tree with food and water

---

21. Bauckham, *Climax of Prophecy*, 350–71.
22. Bauckham, *Climax of Prophecy*, 368–69.

for everyone. All who are thirsty are invited to come to drink freely of the water of life as a gift (22:17). At the end of his revelation, John replaces an economy of exclusion with one where all are fed and given water freely, a radically different vision of provision.

The author of the book of Revelation looks out at the world around him and sees an economy of consumption and luxury, one of economic lust. It left out the vast majority of the empire. As John surveyed this landscape, he came to the conclusion that this was a complete affront to God's desires. He could only explain it as the work of Satan. Thus his response: God is coming soon to put an end to it all and to rescue the righteous.

Revelation should scare us, but not because of its dragon, beasts, and predictions of the future. It should scare us because Rome's economics do not look all that different from today. We stuff ourselves with things we don't need and occupy our free time with needless dainties. We rarely think, or are given the opportunity to know about, the consequences of where our niceties come from. Although John wrote two thousand years ago, his challenge should meet us afresh.

A few years ago, my university hosted a conference on the topic of the Bible and justice. One of our keynote speakers was Elsa Tamez, a scholar who was born in Mexico and had spent time in Columbia and Costa Rica. In her keynote address, she discussed the way in which our economy sucks us in to thinking that things are necessary when they really are not. Things become something we cannot live without. Tamez repeatedly turned to the phrase "mimesis of desire." I find this a chilling phrase to apply to our world today. Mimesis refers to the process by which one thing mimics another. It is a vicious circle of repetitive, learned behavior. The "mimesis of desire" means that we get addicted to things that are embedded in our economy through the lie that they are necessary because we want them. A plutocrat in Rome lounging among his guests may have seen his scented wood, a bronze mirror, or silk garments to be a necessity. We see our smartphones, our SUVs, or large homes as necessities. We desire them because others have them, and we are free to do what we want with our money. The book of Revelation helps us to see the evil aspects of the economy embedded in our lives. We can't see the devil pulling the strings behind the scenes.

If you take our smartphones as an example, their production exploits the extreme poor in many countries of the world.[23] Buying them contributes to the profit margins of the world's largest companies, exacerbating

---

23. Frankel, "Cobalt Pipeline."

the gap between rich and poor. You might say something like this: "But a phone isn't a luxury item, it's a necessary tool in today's world." John would scoff at such a notion. Our sense of a smartphone's necessity only indicates the extent to which we have bought into the lies of our economic system.[24] There is no doubt that they can do a lot of good. The question is, at what price? John (and Luke and Amos) would ask us today: who gets trampled so we can enjoy our iPhones?

Conclusion

Pope Francis, in *Evangelii Gaudium*, approvingly quotes John Chrysostom: "not to share one's wealth with the poor is to steal from them and to take away their livelihood. It is not our own goods which we hold, but theirs."[25] We have looked at three different parts of Scripture that would agree with such a statement. In doing so, we found remarkable consistency in their profiles of a God whose primary interest is in the poor and the lowly. These biblical texts testify that God cares not just about cultivating our faith, but that it also matters what we do with our money. One is not a spiritual thing and the other economic. Money and faith are completely entwined together. You can't say you care for the poor, even if you're very generous with your money, and then go dawdle with your iPhone unthinkingly. (I'm as guilty of this as anyone.)

The first place Pope Francis went outside of Rome after his election was to visit Lampedusa, an island in the Mediterranean where many migrants and refugees from Africa first land in their attempts to enter Europe. Using an altar made of an old fishing boat, the pope said that the death of so many in this watery passage was a thorn in his heart.[26] He said that these people, the poorest of the poor, the most desperate of the desperate, were victims of a selfish society sliding into a "globalization of indifference." He said that people need to "remove the part of Herod that lurks in our hearts."[27] This is an image taken from the Gospel of Matthew, in which Herod orders the death of all infants under the age of two in his attempt to kill Jesus along

---

24. There is evidence that smartphones impact us deeply in our brains and change our behavior: Davey and Davey, "Assessment of Smartphone Addition"; and Tossell et al., "Exploring Smartphone Addiction."

25. Francis, *Evangelii Gaudium*, 57.

26. Allen, *Francis Miracle*, 152.

27. Francis, "Homily of Holy Father Francis," para. 8.

with them. Suggesting that we have Herod in our hearts, in a globalized context, means that the poor are oppressed because of our indifference, and that we kill Jesus along with the migrants.

Bill O'Reilly, in the interview with Candida Moss, uses the phrase "Give to Caesar what is Caesar's and to God what is God's" as evidence that Jesus doesn't want to get into politics. It might seem like Jesus is suggesting that there are religious and political spheres and the two should be kept separate. Such an interpretation is possible, but not likely; the details from the ancient world may indicate something different. Roman coins were implements of propaganda, often with a stamp of Caesar's head and an inscription lauding him as the son of god. When the Pharisees ask Jesus about paying taxes, their intent is to trap him (Mark 12:13). Jesus, however, asks, "Whose head is on the coin?" Jesus has no denarius, but the Pharisees do. They may be guilty of breaking the commandment against graven images. By asking whose face is on the coin, Jesus does not avoid politics, but makes politics explicit. When he says "Give to the emperor the things that are the emperor's, and to God the things that are God's," he is suggesting that where one spends his or her money will reveal their allegiances. Ched Myers makes this clear in his interpretation of Mark when he says that "there are simply no grounds for assuming (as so many bourgeois exegetes do) that Jesus was exhorting his opponents to pay the tax. He is inviting them to act according to their allegiances."[28]

In the opening weeks after he was elected pope, Francis proclaimed that he wanted "a poor church for the poor."[29] In *Evangelii Gaudium*, he quotes from Pope Benedict XVI that there can be no doubt that the "poor are the privileged recipients of the Gospel."[30] John Allen says that Francis's emphasis on these economic issues amounts to his offering a new ecclesiology. An emphasis on economic issues as a component of faith has deep roots in the Bible. These are not the places, however, where the church has always focused its understanding of faith. Pope Francis aims to correct that. The poor and the marginalized are where individual believers, and the church as a whole, need to fill their lungs with the oxygen of the gospel.

---

28. Myers, *Binding the Strong Man*, 312.
29. Allen, *Francis Miracle*, 136–38.
30. Francis, *Evangelii Gaudium*, 48.

4

Francis's Environment: Care for Creation

> All of us . . . are called to watch over and protect the fragile world in which we live.[1]

WHEN IT COMES TO scientific information, Roman Catholics (and, I would add, all Christians) are called to use their God-given intellects to understand evidence as thoroughly as possible. Science is not perfect. Its experts can make mistakes. It is driven, nevertheless, by a desire for truth. It presents to us a certain way of knowing the world even if it may contrast with other ways of knowing. As we will discuss in chapter 8 of this book, experiential ways of navigating the world are also very important. Nevertheless, without science, our knowledge of the world around us, and thus God, would be diminished.

When it comes to the ecological sciences, many people in modern society have a hard time accepting accurate facts. This may be partly due to our social circles, which often have more influence over our opinions about the world than facts do.[2] Lack of concern about environmental problems results from the fact that many of the consequences of a rapidly changing climate will have their full impact at a point in the future, which makes it harder for people today to see its consequences. Moreover, the current impact of climate change is felt more acutely in third-world countries, those without the infrastructure or wealth to mitigate the problems, thus distancing middle- and upper-class America from it effects. Environmental

---

1. Francis, *Evangelii Gaudium*, 216.
2. Kahan et al., "Polarizing Impact of Climate Science," 732.

degradation is removed from us, either chronologically or spatially, so that it is hard to see its immediate consequences.

Pope Francis's encyclical, *Laudato Si'*, calls for an end to such selfish and myopic thinking. The entire first section of this encyclical focuses specifically on what science tells us is happening to our planet. He focuses on pollution and climate change; water pollution and shortages; the loss of biodiversity; social decline; and global inequality. These constitute a global crisis. Humanity's response has been rather "weak," even as the earth itself, and the "abandoned of our world . . . cry out" for a response.[3] There are myriad reasons for the problem, such as weak leadership and the broad selfishness of humans in their daily actions and choices. In general, however, Francis suggests that "we still lack the culture needed to confront this crisis."[4] Francis here builds upon the work of his predecessor, Benedict XVI, who was dubbed the "green pope."[5] In a general audience address in 2009, Benedict XVI offered a statement that might work well as a summary of Francis's view:

> The created world, structured in an intelligent way by God, is entrusted to our responsibility and though we are able to analyze it and transform it we cannot consider ourselves creation's absolute master. We are called, rather, to exercise responsible stewardship of creation, in order to protect it, to enjoy its fruits, and to cultivate it, finding the resources necessary for every one to live with dignity.[6]

This chapter seeks a biblical vision for how we should treat the environment. But here we encounter a significant problem. The Bible has a horrible environmental legacy. To take just one example, Christians have tended to interpret the "dominion" given to humanity by God in Genesis 1:26–28 as giving us carte blanche to do whatever we would like to the planet. Many other parts of Scripture perpetuate an anthropocentric understanding of the environment. In addition, biblical authors did not have the benefit of our modern ecological sciences to understand environmental change with the precision we have available to us today.

In this chapter, we will see the Bible's mixed potential contribution to treatment of the environment. There are many texts that fetishize the destruction of wilderness and view the world in an anthropocentric way (i.e.,

3. Francis, *Laudato Si'*, 53.
4. Francis, *Laudato Si'*, 53.
5. Squires, "Benedict XVI."
6. Benedict XVI, "General Audience," para. 3.

focused on humans alone). On the other hand, some texts exhort humans not to place themselves above the rest of creation, which means we should care for the environment and not destroy it. In the end, by looking at texts such as Genesis, parts of the Psalms, Job, and the Gospel of Mark, we will find the Bible calling for three things: (1) an ecological conversion; (2) a need to engage in politics; and (3) a call to tame the beast within us that drives destruction of the planet.

What Does It Mean to "Have Dominion?"

We begin at the beginning. In the first of two creation myths at the beginning of Genesis, God creates in a very orderly way. Each day resounds like a hymn with the details of what God created, culminating in the refrain that God found it good. These details of creation reach their zenith in the creation of humanity. Woman and man are created simultaneously in God's image and then are given direction on how to manage what God had created:

> Then God said, "Let us make humankind in our image, according to our likeness; and let them have dominion over the fish of the sea, and over the birds of the air, and over the cattle, and over all the wild animals of the earth, and over every creeping thing that creeps upon the earth." (Gen 1:26)

God implements this plan two verses later, speaking directly to the newly created humans:

> God blessed them, and God said to them, "Be fruitful and multiply, and fill the earth and subdue it; and have dominion over the fish of the sea and over the birds of the air and over every living thing that moves upon the earth." (Gen 1:28)

These directions have fed human dominance of creation. They launched a "fairly consistent" trajectory of interpretation across the centuries, buttressed by Greek ideals of human "uniqueness and superiority over the rest of nature."[7] Genesis 1 is not the only place where the idea of dominion over the earth is found in the Bible. Although a different Hebrew word is used, Psalm 8 expresses a similar sentiment. In a context of praise for God as creator, it lauds humanity as the pinnacle of God's creation, those whom God made "a little lower than God" (Ps 8:5), exemplified in the fact that:

---

7. Bauckham, *Living with Other Creatures*, 20. Bauckham does also point out some counterexamples to this phenomenon.

> You have given them dominion over the works of your hands;
>   you have put all things under their feet,
> all sheep and oxen,
>   and also the beasts of the field,
> the birds of the air, and the fish of the sea,
>   whatever passes along the paths of the seas. (Ps 8:6–8)

In 1967, Lynn White had texts such as these in mind when he laid the blame for our modern ecological crisis at the feet of the Christian tradition. Humans, he says, are "conditioned by beliefs about our nature and destiny—that is, by religion." All of the best ecological science in the world, White claims, will not solve the problem because religion will intervene to perpetuate destruction of the environment. He goes on to say, "more science and more technology are not going to get us out of the present ecologic crisis until we find a new religion, or rethink our old one."[8] One might call the command from God to have dominion over the earth as the "original sin" in an environmental sense. It gave the Christian tradition a divinely ordained right to trample and exploit the earth as we see fit.

Some have sought to solve Lynn White's challenge by reinterpreting the concept of dominion in Genesis, seeing it instead as a call for stewardship.[9] In such a move, humans can't do whatever they want because stewardship entails a burden of protection and cultivation. While shifting from "dominion" to "stewardship" might seem a good way out of the problem, it still defines the flourishing of the natural world through a human lens; it remains anthropocentric. The concept of stewardship also does not cohere well with a true understanding of wilderness, places devoid of human footprint. Richard Bauckham asks whether we as humans can "learn to care without interfering, simply to keep away and to keep our hands off, and to do so not so that we still have wildernesses to visit as eco-friendly tourists, but actually because God's other creatures have their own value for God and for themselves, quite independently of us."[10]

James Limburg has taken a different approach to the problem of dominion in the book of Genesis. Limburg begins by noting how many segments of our society ground their desired ethical behavior in God's giving dominion to humanity. For example, hunters in South Dakota claim their

---

8. White, "Historical Roots," 1205–6.

9. Hall, *Imaging God*. Attempts to find stewardship in Genesis 1 go back at least to the seventeenth century (see Bauckham, *Living with Other Creatures*, 58–59).

10. Bauckham, *Living with Other Creatures*, 62.

right to kill foxes in order to increase the population of pheasants. On the other hand, ecologists claim "dominion" as the primary virus in our ecological disease. Since the word is being used on both sides of the debate, Limburg suggests that theologians ought to insist that the word be given "a fair hearing," by which he means we do our best to understand what the biblical author intended by using the word "dominion."[11] He engages in what scholars call a "word study" to try to determine, as best as possible, what the word dominion meant in its ancient context.

The word for "dominion" in Genesis 1:26 and 28 is the Hebrew word *radah*. The word *radah* appears nineteen times in the Hebrew Bible, and, as Limburg points out, it almost always refers to human relationships of power. He notes further that the word is used in discussion of the rule of kings. It is a royal word. This suggests that the author of Genesis intends the human/earth relationship to be modeled on a king/people metaphor. When we look at the other places in the Hebrew Bible where *radah* is used, the texts always have a specific understanding of what the king's rule is supposed to be like. For example, Psalm 72 offers a template for the relationship between a king and his people:

> May he have dominion from sea to sea,
>   And from the River to the ends of the earth . . .
> For he delivers the needy when they call,
>   the poor and those who have no helper.
> He has pity on the weak and the needy,
>   and saves the lives of the needy.
> From oppression and violence he redeems their life;
>   and precious is their blood in his sight. (Ps 72:8, 12–14)

This Psalm offers a specific definition of the word "dominion." It makes clear that dominion does *not* mean domination in any way the king sees fit. Dominion places a burden upon the king to act with justice and care for those who are weak and needy.[12]

If we return to Genesis 1 with this definition of dominion, a new environmental reading emerges. Proper "dominion" would mean care for and help for the ruler's subjects. As Limburg summarizes: humans are "charged to care for the fish, the birds, the cattle, even the earth itself. Far from advocating or even allowing an attitude of exploitation . . . the Genesis

---

11. Limburg, "What Does It Mean," 221–23.
12. Limburg finds this same dynamic operative in Ezekiel 34:2–4 as well.

injunction is a call for the care of the earth."[13] This is an interpretation with which Pope Francis wholeheartedly agrees. He notes that the understanding of dominion has at times led to the "unbridled exploitation of nature." This, he says, "is not a correct interpretation of the Bible as understood by the Church."[14] He admits that, at times, Christians have "incorrectly interpreted" the Bible, but today we must "reject the notion that our being created in God's image and given dominion over the earth justifies absolute domination over other creatures."[15]

Francis finds his own interpretive way out of the problem of dominion by turning to the image of tilling and keeping a garden, from Genesis 2:15. For Francis, these words indicate a "relationship of mutual responsibility between human beings and nature."[16] He frames this in a broader way theologically, making it clear that we are not God and that the earth ultimately is the Lord's (Ps 24:1).

Can attempts such as these, seen in Limburg and Pope Francis, to reinterpret the language of dominion in Genesis be of help? I have spoken to environmental ethicists who claim that the negative understanding of dominion has such a long tradition and has proved so damaging that it is too late to reinterpret the text. Perhaps because I'm trained as a biblical scholar, I am not willing to give up so quickly. Reading "dominion" in Genesis as giving license to destroy and exploit is wrong exegetically (that is, it is not what the author intended it to mean); it is also wrong theologically (that is, it ignores Francis's point that it elevates us too high, forgetting God's ultimate power and role as creator and ruler of the earth). A proper understanding of dominion from the biblical texts should actually place a burden of responsibility on humanity that we care for and nurture nature, allowing it to flourish on its own terms. While these findings cannot undo thousands of years of problematic interpretation, that does not mean we should just give up. We can proceed with a new understanding, one in which dominion places on humanity a burden of care and love for those things over which we have been given power.

13. Limburg, "What Does It Mean," 223.
14. Francis, *Laudato Si'*, 67.
15. Francis, *Laudato Si'*, 67.
16. Francis, *Laudato Si'*, 67.

Are Humans the Center of Creation?

As we noted above, one of the hallmarks of the creation accounts in Genesis 1 and 2 is their focus on humanity as the culmination of God's creation. While there are many important theological aspects of humans being created in the image of God, this idea has also created an unfortunate environmental legacy. If humans sit above creation with dominion, then don't we have a right to subject the environment to our every whim?

A wrong understanding of dominion has led to "anthropocentrism," an assumption that humans are at the center of the natural world. Environmentalists rightly point out the problems created by anthropocentrism. They outline the need not to view nature through a human lens and that we should allow the natural world to flourish without human intervention.[17] The Bible itself, in certain places, does exactly this. There are several key points at which humans are not the culmination of creation, and some in which humans are completely omitted. The best example of this is in the book of Job.

Creation Devoid of Humanity in the Book of Job

Job is a book that comes from Israel's wisdom literature. It is a profound book that deals with the problem of undeserved suffering. The book squirms underneath difficult questions about what can be known about God and God's will. The book of Job suggests that there is an element of uncertainty in a human's interaction with God. When we read Job with an ecological lens, the final chapters of this book add another layer to our understanding of the book.

Most of the book of Job is a conversation between Job, who has suffered greatly, and his friends. Job consistently critiques God for being unjust or absent, while his friends urge patience or accuse him of having done something wrong to deserve his situation. For most of this conversation, God remains silent. At the very end of the book, God finally appears from a whirlwind and speaks. The content of God's response focuses solely on God's role as the creator. In many ways, this is a response to Job's consistent challenges to God. Job had questioned God's omniscience (Job 10:3–6) and God's justice (e.g., 6:1–13). As part of Job's probing of his suffering, he

---

17. This is a particular emphasis within the movement known as "deep ecology." See Naess, "Basics of Deep Ecology," 61–71.

repeatedly turns to images from creation to help make his point. In chapter 9, Job responds to this friend Bildad, who suggested that Job should search out history to find an example of a righteous man who had suffered so badly as Job had (8:1–10). Job's response is to frame his experience from the perspective of God as the all-powerful creator. One cannot contend with God one time in a thousand because God is the one who shakes mountains, who commands the sun, and

> who alone stretched out the heavens
> and trampled the waves of the Sea;
> who made the Bear and Orion,
> the Pleiades and the chambers of the south;
> who does great things beyond understanding,
> and marvelous things without number. (Job 9:8–10)

Job's point here is that God is a big, great, and powerful creator and therefore can do whatever God wants. There is no way to predict what God will do: "he destroys both the blameless and the wicked" (9:22).

Job returns to the created realm in chapter 12. Here he repeats his assertion that he is suffering innocently, claiming that he has done nothing wrong to deserve his suffering. This fact should be so obvious that even a fish could tell you that this is the case:

> But ask the animals, and they will teach you;
> the birds of the air, and they will tell you;
> ask the plants of the earth, and they will teach you;
> and the fish of the sea will declare to you.
> Who among all these does not know
> that the hand of the LORD has done this? (12:7–9)

Job here is suggesting that his friends, who repeatedly suggest that history will prove Job wrong (e.g., 4:7–8; 8:1–10; 15:18–20), have an incomplete view of history. Any recounting of God's history must include a full account of God's creation as well. If we take a proper view of history that encompasses all of creation (not just humanity), then Job will be vindicated. Job seems to be proud of this theological framing of his suffering, grounding it in God's role as creator and ability and power to do whatever God wants. Job thinks this puts everything into a proper perspective and explains what has happened to him: that God treats people randomly and in a way that is not predictable. Who knows such facts, Job claims, better than the animals?

Although Job has taken a step in the right direction, it is even worse than Job thought. He had some insight by suggesting that contemplation of creation could lead to a proper understanding of God's actions. Job was right to think that something can be learned from creation, but he has learned the wrong lesson. When God shows up and finally speaks, humans are absent from God's description of creation. Humans are not even an afterthought; they're not a thought at all.

God first speaks in chapters 38–39 about cosmic aspects of creation. To understand the imagery, we need to know something about the ancient conceptions of the cosmos. At the time of Job, people thought the sky was like a dome over the earth and the land was surrounded by water. They conceived of openings in the dome of the sky from which God would send the rain, snow, and hail. The sun, moon, and stars moved along courses in the dome of the sky. The land on the earth was built on deep foundations. God's response to Job begins by asking him questions about these structures of the cosmos:

> Where were you when I laid the foundation of the earth? (38:4)
>
> Where is the way to the dwelling of light? (38:19)
>
> Have you entered the storehouses of the snow? (38:22)
>
> Can you send forth lightnings? (38:35)

These questions amount to God mocking Job for having no knowledge of the springs of the deep, the origins of light and darkness, and the places from which the snow, hail, and rain emerge. Then the imagery turns to animals, with God asking Job a string of questions there is no way he could answer:

> Do you know when the mountain goats give birth? (39:1)
>
> Is the wild ox willing to serve you? (39:9)
>
> Is it by your wisdom that the hawk soars? (39:26)

All of these things respond, at one level, to Job's knowledge. He thought he knew something, but it turns out he knew vastly less than he thought. Part of his limited ken is his understanding of the natural world. Unlike what he thought, "Job is not the unique reference point for all God's purposes in his creation."[18] The whole of God's bragging about creation is completely devoid of humanity altogether. Unlike Genesis 1, which culminated in the creation

---

18. Bauckham, *Living with Other Creatures*, 8.

of humans, here they have no place at all. If we asked the animals, as Job suggests (12:29), the owl's hoot would be "who?"

God's response to Job ignores Job's complaint. God does not condescend to answer any of Job's questions. At no point is the purpose of earth, its creation, and God's sustenance of it defined in relationship to human beings. As Norman Habel states, "God's answer from the whirlwind is not a defense of heaven but a new understanding of Earth."[19] God revels in creation's expansiveness and explosiveness. Everything from deer calves to sea monsters are part of the natural world, constituent of an understanding of the earth that is good, amazing, and impressive independent of human care, cultivation, or even existence. Creation in Job is rabidly non-anthropocentric.

Pope Francis critiques what he refers to as a "tyrannical anthropocentrism" in which humans are unconcerned for other creatures.[20] This seems in step with God's response in Job. The edifice of our civilization has been built upon an anthropocentric view of nature, in which the things of the earth, from plants to animals to oil, have no intrinsic value in and of themselves. These things derive value only in terms of their utility to humans. The book of Job suggests to us that God may think otherwise. If we truly consider ourselves to be created in the image of God, then perhaps we ought to attempt to view the universe the way God does in Job, where all of creation is equally good, and the place of the humans within it is no different than any other created thing. In the face of human arrogance, the book of Job offers the lingering laugh of the ostrich (Job 39:18).

God as Creator

One of the challenges for the Christian in the modern world is to embrace the learning science provides while maintaining the traditions of faith. This is perhaps most difficult in understanding God as creator in the age of science. The Roman Catholic Church, for example, embraces scientific explanations for the origin of humans: "The question about the origins of the world and of [humanity] has been the object of many scientific studies which have splendidly enriched our knowledge of the age and dimensions of the cosmos, the development of life-forms and the appearance of

---

19. Habel, "Earth First," 77.
20. Francis, *Laudato Si'*, 68.

[humanity]."[21] Most mainline Protestant churches would affirm something similar about science and human origins. The challenge for the thinking, believing Christian is to find a way for such scientific learning not to undermine a belief in God as the creator. In an address to priests, deacons, and seminarians in 2008, Pope Benedict XVI proclaimed that "in recent decades, the doctrine of Creation had almost disappeared in theology; it was almost imperceptible. We are now aware of the damage that this has caused."[22] Pope Francis here would agree that any properly Christian ethic on treatment of the environment must retain a robust sense of God as the creator and the entire cosmos as God's creation.

The challenge of cultivating a robust doctrine of creation is the simplistic notions most Christians have about what the Bible says about creation. The Bible tells us nothing about *how* God created the world. Its texts that discuss creation are mythological and theological, not historical and scientific. When we learn about the natural world, however, we learn something about God. Francis grounds his call for environmental activism in a God who chose to create through evolution and the big bang. The universe is open and shaped by "intercommunicating systems." This means that the whole universe is open to God's transcendence, and that it develops within that transcendence. In creating a world that needs development, God, in a sense, limits God's own freedom. This is because, in a world that is evolving, God wishes "to work with us" and "counts on our cooperation."[23] Following Francis's lead, then, we will explore two Psalms that feature God's role as creator to see what can be gleaned from them with regard to environmental ethics.

Psalm 104—Continuous Creation

One may not be surprised to turn to the Psalms and find God's role as creator as a recurring theme. The Psalms are a compilation of songs and poetry that were sung and recited in a wide variety of occasions, many of which are liturgical. They were written for pilgrimage, weddings, and coronations, and often reflect personal situations of introspection, suffering, illness, or guilt. Many of them are simply hymns of praise.

---

21. *Catechism of the Catholic Church*, 283.
22. Benedict XVI, "Meeting of Benedict XVI with Clergy."
23. Francis, *Laudato Si'*, 80.

Psalm 104 is a *tour de force* in its depiction of God as creator. It begins (vv. 1–9) with God enthroned and clothed with light, the one who stretched out the heavens like a tent and rides the clouds like a chariot. God is then described as the one who keeps the waters at bay by setting its boundaries. These images are borrowed from other ancient conceptions of God, combining language and images that come from the sun god of Egypt and the storm god of the ancient Canaanites.[24] This context helps us understand the opening nine verses of Psalm 104. They not only praise God for creation, but do so in a way that underscores God's extreme power, usurping the images of power used by other cultures of its day.

The next section of the Psalm (vv. 10–30) turns to God's providence for the creatures of the earth. God makes water to flow in the valleys and between the hills, giving water to all the animals. Likewise, God causes the growing of grass and plants that provide food for animals and people:

> You cause grass to grow for the cattle,
>   and plants for people *to use*,
> to bring forth food from the earth,
>   and wine to gladden the human heart,
> oil to make the face shine,
>   And bread to strengthen the human heart. (Ps 104:14–15; italics added)

The phrase "to use" could also be translated as "for people's work" (as in the New American Bible). Whether we "use" or "work with" the goods of the earth might impact the ecological implications of this psalm. If we simply "use" the goods of the earth, humans are little more than hunter/gatherers who take the goods of the earth as they are needed. But if the goods of the earth are "for people's work," the psalm would envision a more invasive role for human cultivation and agriculture. How we translate the original language can have an impact on its ecological implications in our world today. In either case, the psalm seems interested in framing the work of humans broadly within God's role as creator. Whether we "use" or "use for production" the goods of the earth, neither of these activities can be divorced from the fact that they ultimately are God's goods, that God caused them in the first place.

The psalm continues with a panoply of references to created phenomena. The recurring theme is God's control and providence. The sun knows when it is supposed to rise and set, a marked regularity. The workings of

---

24. Dion, "YHWH as Storm-God," 43–71.

creation—their order, predictability, and fecundity—are all examples of God's wisdom (104:24). The psalm references a remarkable variety of plants and animals: trees, cedars, storks, wild goats, lions, and creeping things. From an ecological point of view, there is an understanding here of the marvelous workings of the planet, all as God intended it. One could infer that any disruption to these workings would disrupt the creative intentions of God. Any change to the course of a stream or the destruction of habitat for animals would disrupt the way God intended things to work. Thus, all humans, animals, trees, and hills are dependent upon God. A proper understanding of God as creator should cause us to view the created world (nature) from God's point of view, praise God for that creation, and do nothing to disrupt or harm it.

Finally, it is important to the understanding of Psalm 104 that God's work as creator is not something that was a one-time thing in the past. The psalm points out that God's work continues, that creation consistently relies upon God's creative power, and that everything is constantly being made new:

> These all look to you
>   to give them their food in due season;
> when you give to them, they gather it up;
>   when you open your hand, they are filled with good things.
> When you hide your face, they are dismayed;
>   when you take away their breath, they die and return to their dust.
> When you send forth your spirit, they are created;
>   and you renew the face of the ground. (Ps 104:27–30)

The language of God creating and God's spirit are the same words used in Genesis 1 about creation. They testify to God's ongoing creation, that everything is fragile and all life hangs in the balance. All of creation is dependent upon God's ongoing providence. Creation is continuous.

Psalm 148—All Creation Praises God

Psalm 148 is another Psalm that focuses on God's creation. Here all the elements of the universe are called to praise God: sun, moon, and stars; sea monsters; hail, snow, frost, and wind; mountains and hills; wild animals and cattle; and birds and creeping things. These elements of creation are presented almost as if they had independent personalities and wills of their own. This was not uncommon in the time period, and becomes even more pronounced in some later Jewish literature. This psalm, in a way not unlike the account of creation in Genesis 1, saves humanity for the end:

> Kings of the earth and all peoples,
>   princes and all rulers of the earth!
> Young men and women alike,
>   old and young together! (Ps 148:11–12)

Here the psalm presents humans in the same way that other elements of creation are represented, as part of a poetic song calling for praise of God. The psalm calls attention to opposite pairs of humans: kings and people; women and men; young and old. It is a poetic way of suggesting that no humans are immune from the need to praise God. For our present purposes, it sets a theological agenda for us as we read this text in our environmental situation. We are called to view God first and foremost as creator and to praise God for that creation. There is no hint here of humans somehow being different or extracted from the rest of creation.

Pope Francis claims, in a way that aligns with Psalms 104 and 148, that "the universe as a whole, in all its manifold relationships, shows forth the inexhaustible riches of God."[25] For Francis, this should move our hearts to praise. If we first understand God as creator, then it opens us up to learn about God from God's creation. Such learning is often referred to as "natural theology," an idea that has deep roots in the tradition even though some Christians have occasionally criticized it. Pope Francis sets this natural theology alongside Scripture as an important way that we can know God: "we can say that 'alongside revelation properly so-called, contained in sacred Scripture, there is a divine manifestation in the blaze of the sun and the fall of night.'"[26]

God created the universe, but in a way that is open, that requires ongoing creation. It would seem foolish to stand in the way of the flourishing God intended, as reflected in the Psalms we have explored here. The world God has created, an open-ended universe, is one where all of God's creatures have their role to play. "Creatures exist only in dependence on each other, to complete each other, in the service of each other."[27] This links us together with all the elements of creation in a "sublime communion which

---

25. Francis, *Laudato Si'*, 86.
26. Francis, *Laudato Si'*, 85. Here Francis is quoting from John Paul II.
27. Francis, *Laudato Si'*, 86.

fills us with a sacred, affectionate and humble respect."[28] Any destruction of another part of creation ought to affect us like a wound to our very selves: "God has joined us so closely to the world around us that we can feel the desertification of the soil almost as a physical ailment, and the extinction of a species as a painful disfigurement."[29] All of these observations about the universe and our connection with the rest of creation flow from the foundational observation that God is creator. Our modern understanding of how God creates, informed by the Psalms and science, leads naturally to Francis's call for cooperation. God will work in us and through us, as part of creation, in facilitating creation's destiny.

Jesus and the Environment

Was Jesus a Nature-Loving Hippie?

Several recent treatments of the Bible and the environment try to make Jesus into an environmentalist. These arguments point to how Jesus often used agrarian metaphors in his parables and the fact that there is no sense of a modern throwaway culture in his worldview.[30] Jesus, these authors might claim, "is not driven by an urge to dominate and control the world of nature."[31] Jesus refers to animals and birds, focuses on agriculture, and seems to be partly on a mission to the earth itself.[32]

These points all seem well and good, but they ignore contrary evidence. For example, Jesus was from a small town and likely lived a rural existence. It might not surprise us that he turned to agrarian images in his parables. More importantly, claims that Jesus was in harmony with the earth fit "awkwardly" with stories about Jesus calming a storm, walking on water, or cursing a fig tree.[33] It is far from clear, therefore, whether or not Jesus himself was a helpful advocate for the environment.

---

28. Francis, *Laudato Si'*, 89.
29. Francis, *Laudato Si'*, 89.
30. See, for example, McDonagh, *Greening of the Church*.
31. McDonagh, *Greening of the Church*, 158.
32. Jones, *Jesus and the Earth*.
33. Horrell, *Bible and the Environment*, 65.

Jesus and the Wild Animals in Mark 1:13

Having seen that Jesus may or may not be an ideal environmentalist, it might be helpful to look closely at one particular example from one of the Gospels, to see its potential ecological importance. Here we will explore Jesus's time with the wild beasts mentioned in Mark 1:13.

The Gospel of Mark begins differently than the other Gospels. Matthew and Luke give us ornate birth stories about Jesus. John starts with his famous prologue, proclaiming Jesus as the "the Word." Mark begins breathlessly, with John the Baptist announcing Jesus's arrival and baptizing him, all within a span of just eleven verses. After this, the spirit immediately drives Jesus into the wilderness:

> He was in the wilderness forty days, tempted by Satan; and he was with the wild beasts; and the angels waited on him. (Mark 1:13)

Jesus, to this point, has neither said nothing nor done anything. His ministry begins with a baptism, the heavens wrenched apart (it is a violent word in 1:10), and time in the wilderness with the wild beasts. Mark's Gospel thus begins with images of cosmic disruption, wilderness, and wild animals. There is an ecological component here, but what is it?

To understand Mark's intentions behind the wilderness and wild animals, we need to understand parts of the Old Testament. The Old Testament shows a keen awareness of those places that are suitable for human cultivation and those places that are not, which are deemed the wilderness. The Bible also describes wild forests that, although they provide humans with important resources such as timber, are also the haunt of dangerous animals.[34] Lions, bears, and wild boar all lived in the forests, associating them with danger. These creatures also occasionally left the forest and caused problems for livestock and crops. From the point of view of subsistence farmers in a Bronze or Iron Age society, we can hardly fault them for having negative attitudes toward forests and wilderness, attitudes to which the biblical texts attest.

Despite these occasional negative attitudes, the Old Testament also often offers a vision of the future in which there is a return to Eden, when the barriers between wild places or animals and humans will dissolve. Isaiah 41 offers images in which water and trees will be available in the wilderness. Other parts of Isaiah portray cattle that are able to roam freely without need

---

34. Bauckham, *Bible and Ecology*, 109–11.

for protection from wild animals. Non-biblical texts also fetishize a return to wildness. The end of an apocalyptic text called the "Book of Watchers," which is part of a longer collection of texts known as 1 Enoch, describes a future of uncultivated wilderness. The figure of Enoch, who receives special revelation from God, views scented trees and vast forests and marvels (1 En. 26:6). These wilderness visions offer endless water, food that smells good, and a variety of large beasts and birds. These texts testify that those who curated the Jewish traditions saw a theological problem in the adversarial relationship between humans and nature. These authors suggest that, in a beautiful future crafted by God, the end will be like the beginning.

Finally, the wild animals in Mark 1:13 also bear some exposition in their background. As discussed above, there are many texts in the Old Testament that portray a natural enmity between humans and wild animals. The seeds of such a view may be traced to the expulsion from the garden in Genesis 3:14–19, a text that sets an adversarial relationship between humans and creatures. Other texts testify to something different, a harmonious future in which domestic animals and wild animals are no longer pitted against each other. Most famous here would be the words of Isaiah 11:

> The wolf shall live with the lamb,
>   the leopard shall lie down with the kid,
> the calf and the lion and the fatling together,
>   and a little child shall lead them.
> The cow and the bear shall graze,
>   Their young shall lie down together;
>   and the lion shall eat straw like the ox. (Isa 11:6–7)

Some interpreters have tried to make this text an allegory of peace between nations or groups of people. Although such a reading might work as a "fuller" sense of the text, Richard Bauckham rightly rejects it because there is too much biblical evidence that "relationships between humans and wild animals were a real concern."[35] This relationship was also of theological concern, as the consequences of wrongdoing in Genesis were part of what ruptured this relationship in the first place.

Such future visions of wilderness present a picture of things the way that they should be. Richard Bauckham refers to this as an "ecotopia," because their vision extends beyond just human flourishing, but also "regularly feature the non-human creation and imagine ideal relationships

---

35. Bauckham, *Bible and Ecology*, 121.

between humans and other creatures, both flora and fauna."[36] What can we say, more specifically, about an environmental reading of the opening of Mark's Gospel? There are two options to explore an understanding of Jesus's time in the wilderness with the wild beasts.

Mark 1:13 and Isaiah's Peaceable Kingdom

Mark may mention Jesus and the wild beasts in a way that evokes Isaiah 11 and his peaceable kingdom. The statement that Jesus was "with" the animals hints at no animosity between Jesus and the beasts. Bauckham points out that this is not Jesus domesticating them or exercising dominion; Jesus "befriends" them.[37] Based on the readings of the Old Testament we explored above, recall that in the ancient world, the wild animals were a threat to humanity. As Bauckham states, "wild animals threatened humanity and their wilderness threatened to encroach on the human world."[38] Before Jesus has spoken a single word in Mark's Gospel, Jesus creates a new relationship with the wild animals, one suggesting that the end times will be like the early times; it is almost a return to Eden, where all things live in harmony in a way the creator intended. In this opening image, Mark places Jesus in "ecotopia." Bauckham reads Mark's wilderness scene and our modern context to find a helpful ecological lesson from these verses:

> For us Jesus' companionable presence with the wild animals affirms their independent value for themselves and for God. He does not adopt them into the human world, but lets them be themselves in peace, leaving them their wilderness, affirming them as creatures who share the world with us in the community of God's creation.[39]

Mark's Wild Animals and Ancient Roman Games in the Arena

While I completely agree with Bauckham's conclusion about Mark 1:13, there is another way we could read the ancient context, which could allow us to see a new aspect to Jesus's time with the wild beasts. Bauckham reads the ancient evidence primarily through the Old Testament. In so doing,

36. Bauckham, *Bible and Ecology*, 115.
37. Bauckham, *Bible and Ecology*, 127.
38. Bauckham, *Living with Other Creatures*, 130.
39. Bauckham, *Living with Other Creatures*, 131–32.

he emphasizes the threat that animals in the ancient world posed for humans. There is also evidence, however, of the ways in which humans were a serious threat to animals in the ancient world, which could help us find a different environmental message in Mark 1:12–13.

Environmental historians can trace the impact of human actions on animal populations to time periods long before Jesus. Animal exploitation was particularly acute during the first century CE when Rome's expansion and gladiatorial games resulted in widespread depletion of animal populations. In arenas throughout the empire, Romans killed a mind-boggling number of animals. For example, at the festival opening the Coliseum in Rome (80 CE), there were one hundred days of spectacles. During this time, nine thousand animals were killed. In 108 CE, the emperor Trajan held contests that included nine thousand gladiators, and over eleven thousand animals were killed.[40] The killing of so many animals devastated animal populations in the ancient world. The more exotic and dangerous the animal, the better.

A series of letters between Cicero and his friend Marcus Caelius Rufus demonstrates the widespread destruction of animals. Cicero was governor in Cilicia, a remote province of what is today central Turkey. Rufus was in Rome and needed panthers in order to stage spectacular games there, so he wrote to Cicero to ask him for panthers. Rufus seems to think that the remote location of Cilicia would have them in abundance. Cicero responds that his best hunter came up empty because "there is a remarkable scarcity of panthers."[41] There is no reason to doubt Cicero's words here. In another letter, he laments the loss of human life in the spectacles and asks how it can be fun to watch a wild animal be stabbed repeatedly by a hunting spear. The particular games of which he was speaking saw the death of five hundred lions. Sarah Bond makes a similar point, specifically about crocodiles:

> The Roman Republic saw an unprecedented period of expansion for the Roman empire with many lands being acquired and subjugated. This would result in competitive magistrates increasingly using the games to impress the masses and promote their own personal brand through the display of exotic animals in a kind of fatal zoo-aquarium that was the Roman arena.[42]

---

40. Shelton, *As the Romans Did*, 107.
41. Shelton, *As the Romans Did*, 348.
42. Bond, "Ancient Crocodile Hunters," para. 4.

FRANCIS'S ENVIRONMENT: CARE FOR CREATION

These games were intended to entertain, but they also held significant symbolic value for the Roman Empire. The games took their domination of the earth and made it a microcosm in the arena. The Roman author Plutarch tells a story about the general Pompey and his defeat of the Numidians in Africa. After defeating the enemy, Pompey wanted to make the natives and the animals feel a healthy fear and respect of the Romans, which had been waning:

> He marched through the country for many days, conquered all who came in his way, and made potent and terrible again the Barbarians' fear of the Romans, which had reached a low ebb. Nay, he declared that even the wild beasts in African lairs must not be left without experience of the courage and strength of the Romans, and therefore spent a few days in hunting lions and elephants.[43]

A story like this suggests that Rome benefited from the destruction of animals. Bond makes a similar point about the role crocodiles and Egypt played in the Roman imagination: "those who put on Roman games and paid Egyptian crocodile hunters along the Nile for capturing them fed on the hunger of a Roman audience to see the fantastical beasts at the edges of the newly-acquired bounds of the Roman empire."[44] In other words, Roman propaganda could be expressed through their domination of animals.

The arena demonstrated concretely the power of the emperor and the wealth of those who supported such games. Killing a lion in the center of Rome was a huge expense and was considered by Rome to be "the symbol of their complete power over the universe."[45] Domination over wild animals also underscored social domination. In the games, cruel and destructive animals were eliminated, and the "process showed both how [humanity] controlled nature and how Rome controlled the world."[46] Like the obelisks that Romans brought back from Egypt and erected in their capitol, the "rich variety of animals really illustrated the geographical expansion of Rome's influence."[47]

If we take this information and return to Mark 1:13, the story takes on some new resonances. Although animals were a threat to humans, in the Roman period humans posed an existential threat to many species.

43. Plutarch, *Plutarch's Lives V*, 12.
44. Bond, "Ancient Crocodile Hunters," para. 7.
45. Auguet, *Cruelty and Civilization*, 111–12.
46. Gilhus, *Animals, Gods, and Humans*, 34.
47. Gilhus, *Animals, Gods, and Humans*, 34.

Systematic Roman destruction of wild animals would have been a highly visible component of the empire's propaganda. Jesus establishes a relationship with those things Rome wanted to exploit. The beasts of the earth being extinguished by humanity become the first thing to which Jesus is present and ministers to at the start of his ministry. This suggests that ministering to the earth itself (and not just humans) was integral to Mark's understanding of Jesus's mission. This opening scene for Mark certainly has the idea of "living fraternally with other living creatures," but if we also read it against this Roman background, it has more than a passive edge.[48] It becomes a call to be with those things that are being destroyed, marginalized, and killed. It is no accident that this is the very disposition that Jesus has toward humanity throughout Mark's Gospel as well. He touches the bleeding, the blind, and the dead, those who have been run over or ostracized by society. The opening scene in Mark helps us see that Jesus's mission was not just to humanity. When Jesus describes his life as a "ransom for many" (Mark 10:45), that work extended to all of creation and was not just for humanity.

Conclusion

The Bible has a mixed legacy when it comes to environmental concerns. While it contains beautiful language about God as creator and the world's beauty, it also has images of destruction and anthropocentric texts that could lead to justification of exploitation of the environment. In either case, our current environmental crisis, to which Pope Francis calls such direct attention, puts a burden on us to read biblical texts in light of that crisis. I end this chapter with three insights the Bible provides, in light of those things Francis emphasizes.

Ecological Conversion

Our environmental crisis is not a new one. Humans have been destroying the environment since we became human.[49] It could be that the great migration of humans that serves as the backdrop to the journey of Abraham in the book of Genesis was prompted by ecological changes wrought by

---

48. Bauckham, *Bible and Ecology*, 128–29.
49. See Hughes, *Environmental Problems*.

humans.⁵⁰ Environmental changes could have contributed to the widespread collapse of cultures from which the Israelites first emerged. A long history of environmental destruction by the Greeks and Romans created myriad environmental problems during the time of Jesus and the authors of the New Testament. While we should not think of these authors as environmentalists, it is well within the bounds of reason to expect that environmental factors may be one of the things to which they respond as they formulated their theological understanding of the world. If we think of the biblical texts we have examined in light of these factors, the Bible sometimes offers a radical counter-ideology to that offered by the prevailing culture. Economic systems of greed and exploitation, where final decisions are based on the bottom line, have no place in Scripture. Instead we find a vision of God as creator and the need to care for all of creation. To live in alignment with this vision would be to rethink the very foundations of our society. To think of the other parts of creation, whether flora or fauna, before we think of ourselves, should be the foundation of a biblical environmental ethic.

When read through the lens of our environmental crisis, the Bible ultimately calls for the same thing that Pope Francis does: an "ecological conversion."⁵¹ This conversion must be personal, in the sense of our own spirituality. We must have an "interior conversion" that does not ridicule environmental concerns. What Francis calls for is an ecological conversion "whereby the effects of [our] encounter with Jesus Christ become evident in [our] relationship with the world around [us]. Living our vocation to be protectors of God's handiwork is essential to a life of virtue; it is not an optional or a secondary aspect of our Christian experience."⁵² The breadth of the ways Scripture testifies to this same idea adds depth to Francis's call.

At the same time, personal ecological conversion is not enough. Although it helps, we cannot save the world only by composting, driving a Prius, and taking shorter showers. The problem is too complex to be solved by small individual actions. As Francis says: "Social problems must be addressed by community networks and not simply by the sum of individual good deeds . . . The ecological conversion needed to bring about lasting change is also a community conversion."⁵³ Psalms 104 and 148 are about

50. Hillel, *Natural History of the Bible*, 46–52.
51. Francis, *Laudato Si'*, 216.
52. Francis, *Laudato Si'*, 217.
53. Francis, *Laudato Si'*, 219.

the community of creation. Jesus created community with the wild beasts. Thinking communally, and not just individually, is essential to our future.

Politics?

This chapter began with the assertion that one of the great challenges today for modern Christians is to find a way to think about their faith and to claim God as creator in light of the importance of science. Roman Catholic theology says that there can be no conflict between science and faith, because both are ultimately oriented toward the truth. Science and faith may ask different questions and sometimes seek different answers, but they ultimately are two paths up the same mountain.

The question of the environment is first and foremost a theological and moral question. Our disposition toward creation reveals what we think about God and whether we properly align ourselves with the aims of God. The fact that the Bible and theology are different from science, however, does not mean that we should avoid politics. Christian environmentalists can and should take their convictions to the public square. Pope Benedict XVI made this point clear on several occasions: "The Church has a responsibility towards creation and she must assert this responsibility in the public sphere."[54] The environment is, however, an issue that gets mired in politics all too often. Public policy gets messy. How do we pass laws, make treaties, or sign international agreements in a way that protects our country's sovereignty and yet furthers the flourishing of all life? These are not easy questions to answer. Pope Francis demonstrates a way forward in his address to the United Nations in 2015. While his points are deeply scriptural and should not be controversial for any believing Christian, in a secular setting, he framed the issue much more broadly in his address to the United Nations on September 25, 2015:

> We Christians, together with the other monotheistic religions, believe that the universe is the fruit of a loving decision by the Creator, who permits [humanity] respectfully to use creation for the good of his fellow men and for the glory of the Creator; he is not authorized to abuse it, much less to destroy it. In all religions, the environment is a fundamental good.[55]

---

54. Benedict XVI, *Caritas in Veritate*, 51.
55. *Pope Francis Speaks*, 102.

Francis has demonstrated his interest in engaging in public policy, and both his model and Scripture would call for us to do the same.

Taming the Beast

While there are plenty of scientific reasons to care for the environment, they are no more or less persuasive than the theological reasons. A properly theocentric view of taking care of the environment is one that keeps humans from getting too arrogant and places God's power at the center of our worldview. Pope Francis emphasizes this point in *Laudato Si'*:

> A spirituality which forgets God as all-powerful and Creator is not acceptable. That is how we end up worshipping earthly powers, or ourselves usurping the place of God, even to the point of claiming an unlimited right to trample his creation underfoot.[56]

If we do not have a proper understanding of God as creator, Francis goes on to say, "human beings will always try to impose their own laws and interests on reality."[57] Scripture can help us in this endeavor. It helps decenter the universe from our desire to have it focus on us, to focus instead on the care for those less powerful than us. When Scripture does focus on humanity, it places a burden of care and provision and does not justify exploitation. Proper ethical action cannot simply be self-interested. If we care for the environment simply out of self-preservation, so that humans do not die out, then we are not following a properly biblical environmental ethic. Instead, if we care for the environment because it flows from our worship of God as creator and the worth that God has imbued on all of creation, then we have aligned ourselves with a biblical vision. Then we are, to the extent that we are able, acting like Jesus as he ministered to the wild animals in the Gospel of Mark. Then we truly are with the wild beasts, by taming the beast within.

---

56. Francis, *Laudato Si'*, 75.
57. Francis, *Laudato Si'*, 75.

5

Francis's Blind Spot? Women

> The reservation of the priesthood to males . . . is not a question open to discussion.[1]

ONE YEAR DURING LENT I found myself sitting at a table in our parish activity center eating fish. The conversation turned to the role of women in the church. This topic made the people at the table seem tense, not sure if or how they should speak. But one of them did. I asked her if she would write down what she said that day. Here is what she wrote:

> In nearly any Catholic church, women have proven to be indispensable within their faith communities, conducting Bible studies and major parish programs, leading youth groups and retreats, coordinating and teaching religious education and Vacation Bible programs, orchestrating music liturgy, serving on parish council . . . the list goes on and on. Therefore, it is puzzling to me that the Catholic Church does not seem to believe that women can be as effective as men in leading their church communities in roles as priests.
>
> In many dioceses, the wives of Deaconate candidates have to go through the same classes and training as their husbands but don't have any other role than to support them after that. If they are learning the same things, I would think they are just as qualified to serve in that capacity. Why must they play such a passive role? Aren't women just as capable, and in many cases more capable, of preparing a homily or baptizing a baby than their male

---

1. Francis, *Evangelii Gaudium*, 104.

counterparts? Girls are allowed to be altar servers in many parishes so I guess that's a step in the right direction.

It is disheartening that our children and those of many of our friends are not staying connected to the Catholic faith in which they were raised. Our oldest daughter, who used to be very involved during her formative years, is especially frustrated with the Catholic Church and commented that she would return when they let women be priests. Ouch! Jesus recognized that women had gifts for discipleship at a time when the male-dominated culture of the times was to treat women as inferior. Fortunately the role of women has changed in many ways since Jesus's time. However, the Catholic Church has not kept up with the times.

These comments are not an anomaly. I know from the dozens of first-year students I teach every semester that many women in the church are asking blunt questions that deserve accurate, thorough answers. Many parishioners struggle with the "discomfort" they feel at how the church has handled its teaching on women and ministry.[2]

From the very beginning of his pontificate, Pope Francis began to be asked about the role of women in the church. In an interview with Antonio Spadaro in the fall of 2013, just a few months after his election, it was a major topic of discussion and one that raised eyebrows:

> It is necessary to broaden the opportunities for a stronger presence of women in the church. I am wary of a solution that can be reduced to a kind of "female *machismo*," because a woman has a different make-up than a man. But what I hear about the role of women is often inspired by an ideology of *machismo*. Women are asking deep questions that must be addressed. The church cannot be herself without the woman and her role. The woman is essential for the church. Mary, a woman, is more important than the bishops. I say this because we must not confuse the function with the dignity. We must therefore investigate further the role of women in the church. We have to work harder to develop a profound theology of the woman. Only by making this step will it be possible to better reflect on their function within the church. The feminine genius is needed wherever we make important decisions. The challenge today is this: to think about the specific place of women also in those places where the authority of the church is exercised for various areas of the church.[3]

2. Hudock, "When My Daughter Whispered."
3. Spadaro, "Interview with Pope Francis," 70.

These comments from Francis, so early in his ministry as pope, demonstrate the complexity of the situation. Francis, as had his predecessors, affirms the value and dignity of women. Even as the church has argued that women are not to be ordained as priests, it has always proclaimed their integral mission in the church: "the Church desires that Christian women should become fully aware of the greatness of their mission: today their role is of capital importance."[4] John Paul II claimed that restricting the priesthood to men does not imply that women are of "lesser dignity, nor can it be construed as discrimination against them."[5] So, on the one hand, Francis seems open to rethinking the role of women in the church in a way that shows continuity with his predecessors. On the other hand, Francis's words evince skepticism about the aims of feminism and promulgate an idea known as complimentarianism, which suggests that women and men are fundamentally different and thus not suited for the same roles in society or the church.

As we will see in this chapter, the question of leadership or ordained roles for women in the church is one in which Scripture plays an important role. Unfortunately, we can find problems with how Scripture is used in the church's arguments about women in ministry; there is a need for some critique. At times, the arguments are highly selective and inconsistent. At other times, the church ignores some important evidence.

I personally approach this topic as a faithful Roman Catholic. My goal is to analyze the basis for decisions or arguments that the church has presented. I hope to ascertain the specific role Scripture has played in these documents and decisions. Scripture alone cannot answer all of our questions. The church believes that Scripture and tradition are mutual streams of revelation, that together they form one source. As part of divine revelation, we ought to give Scripture a nuanced and full hearing in the church's discernment of topics as important as ordination and the sacraments.

Closing the Door

How is it that Pope Francis, when asked about women's ordination, can answer so definitively that the "door is closed" or that it is "not a question open to discussion"? The Roman Catholic Church's teaching on women's ordination is far from robust, mostly because this is a recent issue. Rapid

4. Paul VI, *Inter Insigniores*, 6.
5. John Paul II, *Ordinatio Sacerdotalis*, 3

changes in society in the twentieth century, along with new language about the equality between men and women from the second Vatican council (1962–65), created an entirely new context for the modern church. These two factors resulted in an explosion of interest in, and questions about, whether or not women could be ordained in the last fifty years.

In 1973, the US Catholic Bishops published an authorized article in which they discussed some of the traditional arguments for the church's position that women cannot be ordained and suggested that the topic should be given exhaustive study. This document also noted that there was no definitive teaching on the subject. In the summer of 1976, the Pontifical Biblical Commission (a group of scholars whose findings are meant to provide help to the pope) published an appendix on the question, "Can women become priests?" It offers a compendium of observations about women in biblical texts and in ancient society, concluding in part that the New Testament itself will not be able to settle this question definitively. An answer came later that year with the publication of the declaration *Inter Insigniores* by Pope Paul VI, in which he definitively stated that women are not to be admitted into the ministerial priesthood.

Inter Insigniores did not fully set the matter to rest for many leaders in the church, so Pope John Paul II followed up in 1994 with an apostolic letter, *Ordinatio Sacerdotalis*, in which he reiterated what *Inter Insigniores* had said: "I declare that the church has no authority whatsoever to confer priestly ordination on women and that this judgment is to be definitively held by all the church's faithful."[6] One year later (1995), Cardinal Joseph Ratzinger (who would become Pope Benedict XVI) authored what is called a *Responsium ad Propositum Dubium*, which intends to clarify a part of church teaching about which there seems to be some widespread doubt. His letter, which John Paul II signed, asserts the need for "definitive assent" to *Ordinatio Sacerdotalis*, because it has been "set forth infallibly" as part of the Magisterium, the deposit of faith.

These documents are why Pope Francis can so clearly claim that the door is closed to the idea of women's ordination. The papal documents claim that the teaching that women cannot be ordained is based "on the written Word of God, and from the beginning constantly preserved and applied in the Tradition of the church." As we will see, Scripture plays a key role in many of the arguments that these documents make.

---

6. John Paul II, *Ordinatio Sacerdotalis*, 4.

The first part of *Inter Insigniores* to address Scripture extensively is part two, titled "The Attitude of Christ." Here the declaration uses the fact that there were twelve male disciples as a basis for male-only ordination. Its reading of the historical landscape is nuanced. The argument describes how, in light of ancient Jewish and Greco-Roman attitudes toward women—which were generally negative and patriarchal—Jesus acted counterculturally by utilizing women in his ministry. The declaration goes on to say that, when it came time to choose those to whom Jesus would give his "apostolic charge," women were excluded. The logic of the argument suggests that, given Jesus's proclivity to be open toward women in a way contrary to his ancient sociological context, it is all the more meaningful that he decided to choose only men to be among the twelve.

The next section of the declaration turns to the "practice of the apostles." Here it claims that "the apostolic community remained faithful to the attitude of Jesus toward women." The declaration turns to a popular verse, Galatians 3:28, which in the New American Bible reads that "there is neither Jew nor Greek, there is neither slave nor free person, there is not male and female; for you are all one in Christ Jesus." Such a text could be used as an argument in favor of women's ordination. The logic would suggest that in the light of Christ, gender distinctions are rendered moot. *Inter Insigniores* does not prefer this approach. It says: "but this passage does not concern ministries: it only affirms the universal calling to divine filiation, which is the same for all." In other words, Paul was not talking about ordination here, so it is irrelevant in such discussions.

One other way that *Inter Insigniores* argues for an all-male priesthood in light of Galatians 3:28 is by noting the historical fact that Jesus was male: "Nevertheless, the incarnation of the Word took place according to the male sex: this is indeed a question of fact, and this fact, while not implying any alleged natural superiority of man over woman, cannot be disassociated from the economy of salvation." Later church tradition understood Jesus's maleness as an important element of ordination, that the priest stands *in persona Christi* (in the person of Christ) and that there is something essential in the priest being male in order to fulfill that role.

Analyzing the Use of Scripture in *Inter Insigniores*

The use of Scripture in these papal documents, which closes the door on women's ordination, is open to some critique. At times they make dubious claims. At others, they ignore important evidence for which the church has never fully taken account. In this next section, we will examine some of these problems.

Gospels Not Primarily Historical

From a strictly historical point of view, it is possible that Jesus chose only men to be among "the twelve." We must be aware, however, of the nature of the Gospels as historical sources. Three of our Gospels have similar lists of the twelve disciples, whom the texts say Jesus also called "apostles." It is not clear, however, when exactly "the twelve" came to be called apostles.[7] A chronologically earlier reference in 1 Corinthians 15 has Paul referring to them only as "the twelve." Furthermore, the lists of the twelve are not exactly the same in the various Gospels. Mark, the first Gospel written, has a list almost identical to that in Matthew. Luke's list has two different names on it: Judas the brother of James and Simon the zealot. The Gospel of John does not have a definitive list as in the other three Gospels, and some unique names, such as Nathaniel, are attested (see John 1:43–51). These small discrepancies suggest that the primary intentions of the gospel authors were not historical. If they had been, we should expect them to get all the names correct consistently. Finding some differences should not surprise us, however, because as the church document *Dei Verbum* from Vatican II clearly states, the gospel authors wrote with an eye toward the situation of their churches.[8] In other words, their primary goal may not have always been historical. Thus, the declaration on women's ordination does not utilize the individual gospel narratives, failing to acknowledge their individual voices. While none of these lists includes women, their variance presents historical problems for the conclusion that Jesus intended to choose only male apostles. The Gospels are read as if they present a perfectly harmonious historical picture of what Jesus said and did. Given that the lists don't fully agree and that the Gospels are not primarily historical sources, the case lacks certainty.

A bigger problem for the argument in *Inter Insigniores* about Jesus choosing only male apostles is that the Gospels are not the earliest literature we have in the New Testament. The Gospels (and the Acts of the Apostles)

---

7. Fiorenza, *Changing Horizons*, 223–8.

8. "The sacred authors wrote the four Gospels . . . in view of the situation of their churches" (*Dei Verbum*, 19).

were all written between 70 and 100 CE. The earliest literature in the New Testament is the letters written by Paul. The declaration thus treats the material in a way that is not strictly chronological. Most of the names listed as part of "the twelve" in the Gospels are never attested in the letters of Paul. In those letters we also find references to apostles, such as Apollos (1 Cor 4:9), Silvanus, and Timothy (1 Thess 1:1; 2:6), who never appear among "the twelve," and many of whom would never have met Jesus (as Paul himself did not). The exact mechanism for their apostolic charge is not always clear.

Given the nature of the Gospels as sources and their relatively late placement toward the end of the first century, it may be overstated to claim that these four different depictions of the life of Jesus accurately give us "the attitude of Christ" about apostolicity. *Inter Insigniores* does point out that these historical problems "do not make the matter immediately obvious." It claims that a "purely historical exegesis of the texts cannot suffice" when trying to reach the "ultimate meaning of the mission of Jesus and the ultimate meaning of Scripture."[9] The declaration never makes clear what other approach to Scripture is necessary. A historical picture of the practice of the early church suggests a wide variety of origins for early church leadership (not just from those among "the twelve").

When Can We Discuss Ordination?

As we just noted, Paul's letters provide our earliest access to Christianity in the first century. Quite often we see prominent women in the orbit of Paul's ministry. For example, Phoebe (Rom 16:1–2), Chloe (1 Cor 1:10–17), and Junia (Rom 16:7) deliver letters, send reports, or have official titles. *Inter Insigniores* finds this unremarkable because "at no time was there a question of conferring ordination on these women." Moreover, the declaration's reading of Galatians 3:28, discussed just previously, claims that the dissolving of division between male and female is not relevant to discussions about ordination because this text is about baptism and not ordination.

The problem with such statements is that at no point during the entire New Testament period was there a question of conferring "ordination" on anyone. The New Testament never uses the language of "sacraments" at all. It also never uses the words "priest" or "priesthood" in a technical sense for Christian ministry (a point made by Pontifical Biblical Commission in its report). In other words, the declaration erects a standard to which

---

9. Paul VI, *Inter Insigniores*, 2.

no text in the New Testament can live up. The church's understanding of sacraments, including ordination, develop over time and are defined later in the tradition, long after the New Testament period. Trajectories and ideas from Scripture certainly feed later understandings of ordination. But to suggest that ordination is sufficiently codified in the New Testament so as to exclude women does not accurately represent the documents as we have them. The declaration picks and chooses what it wants: when it is men involved, then this clearly gives us insight into the mind of Christ regarding God's call to male-only ordination. When a woman's leadership is present in the New Testament, the declaration does not take it seriously because it can't be "about ordination."

All discussion of ordination in the New Testament is anachronistic. The evidence from the New Testament period suggests that the early church conferred titles—deacon, bishop, elder, apostle—which imbued individuals with a certain status. These are observations that the Pontifical Biblical Commission itself noted when it said that even asking the Bible if women can be ordained is "a way of looking at things which is somewhat foreign to the Bible." Thus, the declaration's decision to say that some texts are about ordination, and others are not, is arbitrary and does not properly pay heed to the historical nature of the source material in the New Testament.

One other way that *Inter Insigniores* argues for an all-male priesthood is by noting the historical fact that Jesus was male: "Nevertheless, the incarnation of the Word took place according to the male sex: this is indeed a question of fact, and this fact, while not implying any alleged natural superiority of man over woman, cannot be disassociated from the economy of salvation." This is obviously an indisputable fact. The question is this: to what extent is Jesus's maleness essential to the economy of salvation insofar as it sets a template for ordination? In those places where early church writers do discuss the role of women, they are not primarily motivated by "the mind of Christ." They tend to start with an idea of the inferiority of women rather than the importance of being male in order for the priest to serve *in persona Christi*.[10] We could also ask whether or not the lack of distinction between male and female in Galatians 3:28 ought to provide context for our understanding of ordination. This text is primarily about what happens to the baptized, envisioning an end to social divisions: male/female; slave/free; Jew/Greek. This is certainly, as the declaration claims, a universal call for all Christians. Do we weaken this truth, however, if we let

---

10. Wright, "Patristic Testimony," 526.

the distinctions remain in our understanding of ordination and salvation? Should we also retain ethnic distinctions (i.e., Jew/Greek) in our understanding of ordination and salvation? Jesus was historically Jewish, as were "the twelve" in the Gospels. Do priests today have to be ethnically Jewish in order to serve *in persona Christi*?

Revisiting Ignored Evidence

There are some figures in the New Testament whom *Inter Insigniores*, and its follow-up letters, never mention specifically. We will now look closely at the letters of Paul and what we know about how his ministry functioned in the ancient world in order to shed light on what *Inter Insigniores* neglects. While Paul occasionally limits roles for women in Christian assemblies (see 1 Cor 14:32–36), other evidence suggests that women were integral. When we get glimpses of Paul's ministry "on the ground," we find women who enjoyed significant leadership roles and who participated in early Christian ministry in a way equal with himself.

At the end of his letter to the Romans, Paul sends greetings to over twenty-five individuals, ten of whom are women. Some of these greetings are to people whom Paul just happened to know, but most of them are recognized for the specific roles they played in the early church. He greets coworkers, those who risked their lives along with him (16:4), and those who worked hard (16:6, 9, 12). Two women here are worth considering with more detail.

Phoebe and Women Deacons in the New Testament Period

Romans 16:1–2 states:

> I commend to you our sister Phoebe, a deacon of the church at Cenchreae, so that you may welcome her in the Lord as is fitting for the saints, and help her in whatever she may require from you, for she has been a benefactor of many and of myself as well.

We learn a lot about this woman Phoebe from these two short verses. She is from Cenchreae, a port city outside of Corinth (Paul visits this city according to Acts 18:18). She clearly has an important role in Paul's ministry. Paul "commends" or "recommends" her to the Romans. This suggests to most scholars that Phoebe may have been the one who delivered the letter for Paul. If she was with Paul at its sending, we may also speculate that she was the letter's first authoritative interpreter. If the church in Rome had questions about what Paul wrote (and they likely did, since it is Paul's longest and most theologically intricate letter), she would have been on hand to help clarify questions from the community. Paul also calls her a "benefactor." This indicates that she provided material wealth to support the church and Paul's network.

If you read Romans 16:1–2 in the New American Bible Revised Edition (NABRE) you will find Phoebe called a "minister" of the church in Cenchreae. If you read the New Revised Standard Version (NRSV), she will be called a "deacon." Other translations call her a "servant." The Greek word that is used here is *diakonos*. This word refers to anyone who is a servant or who serves other people. For instance, in the story of the wedding at Cana in John 2, the word *diakonos* is used to designate the servants at the wedding feast. At some point in the early church, however, the word took on extra significance and became an officially designated title, from which we derive our word "deacon." A few examples from the New Testament will demonstrate the various ways the word *diakonos* can be understood and translated:

- In 1 Corinthians 3:5, Paul uses the word *diakonos* to refer to both himself and Apollos, another well-known early Christian apostle: "What then is Apollos? What is Paul? Servants (*diakonoi*) through whom you came to believe, as the Lord assigned to each." Paul does not use the word here in a technical way, but to describe the character of their ministry. He emphasizes that the nature of their leadership is one of servitude. (Paul uses the word *diakonos* in a similar way in 2 Corinthians 3:5–6.)

- In other places, Paul uses this word in a technical way to refer to people with official standing in the church. For example, in Ephesians 6:21 he states: "So that you also may know how I am and what I am doing, Tychicus will tell you everything. He is a dear brother and a faithful minister (*diakonos*) in the Lord. I am sending him to you for this very purpose, to let you know how we are, and to encourage your hearts." In this case, we see *diakonos* being used quite similarly to Romans 16 when it is used of Phoebe. Paul is commending Tychicus to the Ephesian community as a sanctioned conduit of information (this same information is echoed in Colossians 4:7).

- Paul's letter to the Philippians probably has the strongest evidence that Paul may use *diakonos* as an official and authoritative role in the church. He starts this letter by saying: "Paul and Timothy, servants of Christ Jesus, to all the saints in Christ Jesus who are in Philippi, with the bishops and deacons." Instead of the "bishops and deacons," the New American Bible translates this final phrase as: "with the overseers and ministers." This translation waters down the titles by generalizing them. Given that this is an introduction to the letter, Paul likely has something structural and official in mind. These are Deacons with a capital "D."

A translation of the Greek word *diakonos* as "minister," "deacon," or "servant" will resonate quite differently within the walls of modern churches.

When talking specifically about the Apostle Paul and his letters, we cannot get into his head, nor can we reconstruct exactly how the early church functioned. Given this early period of the church, it might be too much to expect that language and titles would have been used consistently at all times. At some points, Paul clearly seems to use the word bishop and deacon as official titles. At other times, the word *diakonos* simply means a "servant-leader" and could refer to anybody. At this point, the church was fledgling and things were being worked out; not everything was yet codified.

Later in the first century, during the decades after Paul, the situation changed. The First Letter of Timothy lays out specific guidelines for the office of bishop and deacon. By this point, we can say that these words have come to be understood as officially sanctioned leadership roles within the church. The author gives specific qualifications for deacons. They are to be serious, sober, not greedy, and have a clear conscience. The text then seems to assume that women could be deacons: "Women, likewise must be serious, not slanderers, but temperate, faithful in all things" (1 Tim 3:11).[11]

If we return to Phoebe in Romans 16, there is ample evidence from within the New Testament and from what Paul says about her to understand her role as a deacon. Paul uses the word *diakonos* to describe his own ministry (although he uses other words as well) and there are hints in later decades of the first century that women were allowed in such a position (1 Tim 3:8–13). If Paul understood Phoebe as a deacon, she is far from an

---

11. The Greek word for "woman" can be translated as either "wife" or "woman." Because of this, some claim that 1 Timothy is talking about the wives of male deacons, not women deacons. The plain sense of this text, however, suggests that women are able to be deacons. Even the New American Bible translates this as "women" with a footnote saying that the idea of women deacons is to be preferred.

anomaly, someone who slipped through the cracks of an otherwise patriarchal early church. The evidence would suggest the opposite: that she may be an example of a broader phenomenon in the early church.

Given that there likely were women in leadership roles under the title of deacon in the early church, could there be a movement to revive the idea of women in the permanent diaconate today? Pope Francis's comments about a "closed door" apply only to women as priests. In 2016, he commissioned a group to study the possibility of women as deacons. This twelve-member group includes academics and church leaders, some of whom are open advocates for women deacons.[12] Francis has been clear, however, that this is only a study group, as he stated in an interview shortly thereafter: "I then chose those people from the two lists who I thought were the most open and the most competent for the new commission. It was a matter of studying the topic and not of opening a door."[13] We don't know yet where such a commission will lead. Any new movements in the church toward women deacons will have precedent in the New Testament based on its theological understanding of Christian leadership and the fact that women were in such roles early on.

In the United States there would be broad support for women deacons. A 2018 study by America Media found that 60 percent of women in the United States would support the idea of women deacons. Another 21 percent said "maybe" and would be open to learning more. Only 7 percent of those surveyed answered "no" to the question.[14] The church is not a democracy, but there is a broad sense in the church that the lack of women in ordained ministry is increasingly out of step with the implications of the equality between men and women.

Junia: Female Apostle

A few verses after introducing Phoebe, Paul says, "Greet Andronicus and Junia, my relatives who were in prison with me; they are prominent among the apostles, and they were in Christ before I was" (Rom 16:7). The second name in this verse, Junia, is a woman. There is no doubt that Paul understood it that way and that he calls her an apostle. Because of the way that Greek grammar works, when this name was the direct object in a sentence (as it is

---

12. Gajiwala, "Women," 193.
13. Pongratz-Lippitt, "Pope Francis Discusses," para. 7.
14. Gray, "Proud to be Catholic," para. 20.

here), the female and male version of this name look identical. Grammatically speaking, the name could be either male or female in Romans 16:7. As the Bible was read, copied, and translated across the centuries, the name was read as Junias (a male name), thus scrubbing Junia, a female apostle, from the record. The understanding of Junia as a male persisted well into the twentieth century, when the critical Greek texts on which Bible translations are based still wrote the name as a masculine one. More recently, however, scholars have been revisiting this verse and asking whether the second person named is a man (Junias) or a woman (Junia).

In 2005, Eldon Epp published an exhaustive account of Junia and how she was understood in the manuscript tradition of the New Testament. He wanted to know the likelihood of whether Paul thought Junia was a male or a female. His research revealed that there were 250 times that Junia was used as a female name in antiquity. He found zero examples of Junias, the male version of the name.[15] The evidence is clear: Junia was only ever known as a female name in antiquity. There was no male equivalent. In the last forty years, our understanding of this figure has changed thoroughly. It took a while for these changes to make their way into our Bibles, however. When I first started teaching full time in 2007, some students in my classes would have the name "Junias" (the male version) in their Bible, and some would have Junia (the female version). More recently, this is less the case; almost all modern Bible translations now print "Junia," a woman, in Romans 16:7.

At the beginning of section 3, *Inter Insigniores* states: "the apostolic community remained faithful to the attitude of Jesus toward women . . . at no time was there a question of conferring ordination on these women." After noting that Paul does mention some women in Romans 16, the declaration concludes: "In spite of the so important role played by women . . . their collaboration was not extended by St. Paul to the official and public proclamation of the message, since this proclamation belongs exclusively to the apostolic mission." This statement would surely surprise Junia, whom Paul calls an apostle, were she still alive.

Given the time period in which *Inter Insigniores* was written (1976), is it possible that Pope Paul VI did not know about Junia, a female apostle, in Romans 16:7? One could look to an authority from the early church, Saint John Chrysostom (d. 407 CE), who said, "How great the wisdom of this woman that she was even deemed worthy of the apostles' title."[16] Moreover,

---

15. Epp, *Junia*, 54.
16. As quoted in Epp, *Junia*, 79.

Pope Paul VI's own biblical commission mentioned Junia, whom they called "noteworthy" as one who was "placed in the rank of the apostles with regard to whom one or another raises the question of whether it is a man." This assessment, awkwardly phrased, makes clear that Junia is a woman and that only a few scholars do not adopt such an idea.

Readers of English today who open to Romans 16:7 in the Roman Catholic translation, the New American Bible Revised Edition, will find Junia, who is "prominent among the apostles." This woman apostle is in our Bible, but not in our papal documents.

Conclusion

In summary, *Inter Insigniores* ignores some evidence and picks and chooses to make its points as conveniently as possible. What is most striking in this case is that the declaration does not even make use of all of the evidence (about Junia) as presented by its own biblical commission. In the New Testament, and in the practice of the earliest church, women held prominent roles. We have seen evidence of women in the roles of deacon or minister in the early church. In the case of Phoebe, this meant that she was entrusted with Paul's letter to Rome and was charged as its earliest authoritative interpreter. In the case of Junia, a prominent and well-known apostle, she clearly shares the same role as Paul himself and was converted before Paul. There is no higher title that could have been given to her in this earliest period of the church.

What I hope to have offered here is a thorough assessment of the biblical evidence on which the teaching of *Inter Insigniores* is based. Although the church documents intended to put this issue to rest, it clearly has not succeeded. Many people within the church continue to ask questions. It does not feel to them like it is settled. Cindy Wooden, the Rome Bureau Chief for Catholic News Service, recently reported on Twitter the conclusions of the Pontifical Commission from Latin America as saying, "The absence of women in (church) decision making is a defect, an ecclesiological lacuna, the negative effect of a clerical and chauvinistic mentality."[17] The group goes on to suggest that this situation "raises the

---

17. See the following tweet from Cindy Wooden's Twitter account: https://twitter.com/Cindy_Wooden/status/984108074838478850.

question of a synod of the universal church on the theme of women in the life and mission of the church."[18]

It is difficult for people to stop asking the questions that arise from their experience of the church and the world. As Barry Hudock stated in a recent article in *America* magazine: "Wherever you stand on the matter, it should be clear to all of us that the doctrine [of a male-only priesthood] represents a problem for evangelization. Even if the teaching is not unjust—even if it is not the result of the church's failure to fully appreciate the dignity and equality of women—the perception by many, if not most people in the United States today is that it is. And the very perception of an unjust church handicaps its ability to witness effectively to the world."[19]

Does Pope Francis, as some suggest, have a "blind spot" when it comes to issues of women in the church?[20] Francis seems to work from an idea that women are equal in dignity, but that men and women have been given different strengths and abilities. As he said in an interview early in his pontificate, "a woman has a different makeup than a man."[21] Francis also has a concern that women will seek ordination as a means to power, that it might be dominated by "macho categories."[22] Not everyone will agree with such an argument from Pope Francis because, as many women would point out, "it's rather disingenuous to play down the importance of power when you're the one wielding it."[23]

Francis calls for new thinking about the role of women in the church. While the door may be closed to women priests, we have already seen the possibility that women could be ordained as deacons, something that the New Testament evidence would clearly support. Scripture cannot answer all of our questions about sacraments and ordination in particular, but I hope that the variety of leadership roles evident in the New Testament can help stimulate the kind of new thinking for which Francis advocates in the church today:

> I readily acknowledge that many women share pastoral responsibilities with priests, helping to guide people, families and groups

---

18. See the following tweet from Cindy Wooden's Twitter account: https://twitter.com/Cindy_Wooden/status/984108676859379712.

19. Hudock, "When My Daughter Whispered," para. 10.

20. Allen, *Francis Miracle*, 123.

21. As quoted in Allen, *Francis Miracle*, 124.

22. Allen, *Francis Miracle*, 124.

23. Allen, *Francis Miracle*, 125.

and offering new contributions to theological reflection. But we need to create still broader opportunities for a more incisive female presence in the Church. Because "the feminine genius is needed in all expressions in the life of society, the presence of women must also be guaranteed in the workplace" and in the various other setting where important decisions are made, both in the Church and in social structures.[24]

Francis's words here do not sound all that different from those of the parishioner with whom I shared my Lenten fish. She and Pope Francis see the integral role of women already in the church, but also feel the need for something more.

---

24. Francis, *Evangelii Gaudium*, 103.

6

Francis's Task: Becoming Heralds of Mercy

God is pure mercy[1]

ON MONDAY, OCTOBER 14, 2013, Pope Francis gave a daily homily in which he talked about the "Jonah syndrome." The topic of Jonah came from the gospel reading for that day, Luke 11:29–31:

> When the crowds were increasing, he began to say, "This generation is an evil generation; it asks for a sign, but no sign will be given to it except the sign of Jonah. For just as Jonah became a sign to the people of Nineveh, so the Son of Man will be to this generation." (Luke 11:29–30)

Francis points out that these words are directed not at Jesus's followers, but the doctors of the law and Pharisees who show up later in the chapter (Luke 11:37–54). These are the people, Francis claims, who are too attached to doctrine. He calls this the "Jonah syndrome" because it describes "those who have no desire for people to be converted."[2]

Luke's story presumes knowledge of the book of Jonah in the Old Testament. Jonah runs away from God's call to go to Nineveh because he does not want the wicked people there to have a chance to repent: "O LORD! . . . that is why I fled to Tarshish at the beginning; for I knew that you are a gracious God and merciful, slow to anger, and abounding in steadfast love, and ready to relent from punishing" (Jonah 4:2). In other words, Jonah does not follow God's call because of God's graciousness, and

---

1. See the following tweet from the pope's official Twitter account: https://twitter.com/Pontifex/status/371574052818665473.

2. Francis, *Morning Homilies II*, 62.

Jonah does not think the people in Nineveh deserve such merciful treatment. This "Jonah syndrome," Pope Francis says, leads to a self-sufficiency "we think we can attain because we're good, clean Christians, because we do those good works, keep the commandments, all that."[3] The real sign of Jonah, for Francis, is "God's mercy."

Pope Francis's reading of this particular text demonstrates that he views everything through a lens that magnifies the absolute primacy of God's mercy. God's mercy comes before all things and humans are to erect no impediments to it. The story of Jonah also introduces another aspect of how Francis tends to understand mercy: God's mercy is not always directed at "us." The scandal of the gospel, and the core of Francis's understanding of God's mercy, is it being directed toward those we consider to be the "other." In this chapter, we will explore the meaning of the word "mercy" in the Old Testament, particularly in Israel's wisdom literature. Then we will see how it is used in the New Testament with a close analysis of Luke's parable of the good Samaritan.

Mercy as Almsgiving

What does the word "mercy" mean? Where does it come from and how is it used in the Bible? In the Old Testament, there are a variety of words that get translated as the English word "mercy." One important word that sometimes gets translated as "mercy" is the Hebrew *ḥesed*. This is a word most often reserved for God's special relationship with the people, as in Deuteronomy's version of the Ten Commandments, which claims that God will show "steadfast love to the thousandth generation of those who love me and keep my commandments" (Deut 5:9–10). The phrase "steadfast love" here is sometimes translated as "mercy."

When discussing mercy, Pope Francis points to a particular historical time period and type of literature in which biblical authors talked frequently about mercy. The word "mercy" shows up more often in a part of the Old Testament known as the wisdom literature. Books such as Proverbs, Sirach, and Tobit use the concept of mercy frequently. In this literature, mercy was often understood in terms of charity. One could say that in this time period the word "mercy" meant monetary charity toward another.

The book of Tobit provides a helpful example. Tobit is a folk tale that also contains some wisdom sayings passed down from Tobit to his son,

---

3. Francis, *Morning Homilies II*, 63.

Tobias. Tobit's wisdom is dominated by a certain understanding of mercy that brings it into close alignment with acts of charity toward the poor. At the very beginning of the book of Tobit, he describes himself as one enacting mercy: "I, Tobit, walked in the ways of truth and righteousness all the days of my life. I performed many acts of charity for my kindred and my people" (Tob 1:3). The Greek word translated here as "acts of charity" can also mean "mercy."[4] This same word is used in Tobit's prayer in chapter 3 to mean mercy:

> You are righteous, O Lord,
>   and all your deeds are just;
> all your ways are mercy and truth. (Tob 3:2)

In the book of Tobit, the idea of mercy and acts of charity are closely linked. In the next chapter, Tobit's instructions to his son further explicate how the author understood this idea:

> Revere the Lord all your days, my son, and refuse to sin or to transgress his commandments. Live uprightly all the days of your life, and do not walk in the ways of wrongdoing; for those who act in accordance with truth will prosper in all their activities. To all those who practice righteousness give alms [mercy] from your possessions, and do not let your eye begrudge the gift when you make it. Do not turn your face away from anyone who is poor, and the face of God will not be turned away from you . . . for almsgiving [mercy] delivers from death and keeps you from going into Darkness. Indeed, almsgiving, for all who practice it, is an excellent offering in the presence of the Most High. (Tob 4:5–11)

The words for "mercy" and "acts of charity toward the poor" are synonymous here. We are also introduced here to a radical idea, that mercy/almsgiving can *accomplish* something for the one doing it. Mercy can help you in the future and save from death. Later in the book, the claim becomes even more theological, this time in the words of the archangel Raphael:

> Prayer with fasting is good, but better than both is almsgiving with righteousness. A little with righteousness is better than wealth with wrongdoing. It is better to give alms than to lay up gold. For almsgiving saves from death and purges away every sin. (Tob 12:8–9)

---

4. The book of Tobit was originally written in Aramaic. We do not have a full ancient version in that language, however, so our modern Bibles translate it from ancient Greek.

Here the claims for what mercy/almsgiving can achieve goes even higher. Now they are responsible for washing away sin. In his extensive study of this topic, David Downs concludes that, even though such a claim may be shocking, we need to take seriously the idea that there is an "atoning efficacy of almsgiving."[5]

The book of Sirach also discussed the atoning efficacy of almsgiving. Its author claims: "As water extinguishes a blazing fire, so almsgiving atones for sin." (Sir 3:30). Sirach repeatedly expresses such ideas:

> One's almsgiving is like a signet ring with the Lord,
>   and he will keep a person's kindness like the apple of his eye. (17:22)

> Store up almsgiving in your treasury,
>   and it will rescue from every disaster. (29:12)

> Kindred and helpers are for a time of trouble,
>   but almsgiving rescues better than either. (40:24)

We find in Sirach the same sentiment as we saw in Tobit, that "mercy" is synonymous with giving alms and that it directly leads to atonement for sins. Downs summarizes the core components of mercy/almsgiving in this literature:

- Mercy is an essential part of a virtuous life
- Mercy will be "honored and recompensed by God"
- Mercy allows one to receive help in times of trouble
- Mercy "establishes solidarity" among those who give alms
- Merciful deeds effectively atone for sin[6]

Mercy, therefore, is not some wishy-washy idea of being nice to each other. Mercy is not soft. The idea of mercy, according to some parts of the Bible, is the core element in how human beings are saved. For the authors of these texts, mercy is concrete action.

These observations about the overlapping meaning of mercy and giving of alms dovetail quite nicely with how Pope Francis talks about the preferential option for the poor. Francis is quite insistent that the option for the poor—the idea that God has a special place in the divine heart for

---

5. Downs, *Alms*, 70.
6. All in Downs, *Alms*, 81.

the poor—is "primarily a theological category."[7] This means that the idea starts not from cultural, anthropological, or sociological understandings of humanity and the need to help the poor. It starts with a deep knowledge of God, how God views the world, and what belief in God demands. Inspired by such an idea, "the Church has made an option for the poor which is understood as a 'special form of primacy in the exercise of Christian charity, to which the whole tradition of the Church bears witness.'"[8]

What we have seen in the wisdom literature is that the biblical text supports the idea that mercy is a theological category for understanding concrete action in the world for the poor and marginalized. Pope Francis himself quotes from both Tobit and Sirach to support his exposition of mercy in *Evangelii Gaudium*. A couple of examples from the New Testament pick up this same theme. James 2:13, for example, claims that "mercy triumphs over judgment." Francis also turns to Saint Augustine, who offers a vivid story to help explicate the point:

> If we were in peril from fire, we would certainly run to water in order to extinguish the fire . . . in the same way, if a spark of sin flares up from our straw, and we are troubled on that account, whenever we have an opportunity to perform a work of mercy, we should rejoice, as if a fountain opened before so that the fire might be extinguished.[9]

In other words, mercy is like our fire brigade and we can employ it to douse the ever-rising flames of sin. Francis summarizes these points by saying: "This message is so clear and direct, so simple and eloquent, that no ecclesial interpretation has the right to relativize it."[10] The church's interpretation is never allowed to weaken the clear biblical message of mercy understood as work for the poor.

The Good Samaritan—Mercy from Your Innards

The parable of the Good Samaritan (Luke 10:25–37) is one of the best-known stories told by Jesus. This parable, which appears only in Luke's

---

7. Francis, *Evangelii Gaudium*, 198.

8. Francis, *Evangelii Gaudium*, 194. Here Francis quotes John Paul II's encyclical *Sollicitudo Rei Socialis*.

9. Francis, *Evangelii Gaudium*, 193. The quotation is from Augustine's *Catech.* 14.22.

10. Francis, *Evangelii Gaudium*, 194.

Gospel, has an incredible ability to continue to challenge us today and contributes to a scripturally informed understanding of mercy.

The author of the Gospel of Luke is a storyteller. Many of the famous parables that Jesus tells are unique to Luke's Gospel; they are not found anywhere else in the Bible. Luke's parables focus on the lost coin, women lighting lamps, the prodigal son, and the lost sheep. The parable of the good Samaritan comes in chapter 10, near the beginning of the second half of Luke's Gospel. When a story is this familiar, we often lose sight of the details. It can be difficult to find new ways for such a story to challenge us. The analysis here will look closely at the details of this story to try and hear it in a new way.

Meeting the Lawyer

Luke frames the parable with a story about a lawyer who stood up to test Jesus. He asks Jesus what he must do to inherit eternal life. Jesus asks him what the law requires, and the man answers with well-known words from the Old Testament. The first part comes from Deuteronomy 6:5: "You shall love the Lord your God with all your heart and with all your soul and with all your strength." The final phrase of the lawyer's answer comes from Leviticus 19:18: "you shall love your neighbor as yourself." This statement was very important for Jews at the time of Jesus. One rabbi from that time period claims that it was the "greatest teaching of the Torah."[11] Jesus's response to the lawyer's answer was positive: "You have given the right answer; do this, and you will live" (Luke 10:28). But the story does not end here. The lawyer still seems unsatisfied; Luke says that he wanted to "justify himself." It is not exactly clear what such a phrase means. The lawyer may have been preoccupied with his own salvation, preening in what he thinks he knows. Or he may have intuitively sensed that though he gave the textbook answer, the real answer was somehow deeper.

Luke wants us to see this lawyer negatively. He intends to "trap" Jesus, although it's not clear how these questions constitute anything of the sort. Elsewhere in Luke, lawyers are not viewed positively. For example, in chapter 7, Luke mentions that Pharisees and the lawyers refused to be baptized by John the Baptist, therefore rejecting "God's purpose for themselves" (7:30). Also, Luke does not like people who want to justify themselves (see 16:15). Whatever his motivations, the lawyer opens up a

11. Levine, *Short Stories by Jesus*, 89.

new avenue for discussion with his second question to Jesus: "And who is my neighbor?" Jesus responds with a story.

The Parable Itself

During Jesus's time, some interpreted "love your neighbor" to mean love only for other Israelites.[12] The lawyer's question, "who is my neighbor?" is a natural one. When Luke calls the opening character nothing other than "a certain man," he begins to answer the question. Anyone can be a neighbor. By starting with nothing more than "a certain man," Jesus undercuts any inquiry as to whether he qualified as a neighbor or not, a "powerful rhetorical move" by Jesus at the parable's opening.[13] No classification is provided for him, which means no one can ask questions about whose side he would have been on as he writhes beaten and robbed in the ditch.

The next part of the story passes quite quickly. In only two verses we hear of a priest and a Levite passing by the person in the ditch. The interpretation of these two figures in Christian history has unfortunately been dominated by anti-Semitic readings. For some, these two represent typical Jews who were so preoccupied with issues of purity that they did not want to approach the person for fear of defilement. For others, they represented the snobby elite who were too good and didn't want to get their hands dirty.[14] In some early Christian allegorical interpretations of this story, the priest and the Levite represent the law and the prophets, neither of which could heal the man. In such a reading, the Samaritan represents Jesus, who comes along and heals. Ambrose of Milan (d. 397 CE), for example, says this:

> Here the Samaritan is going down. Who is he except he who descended from heaven, who also ascended to heaven, the Son of Man who is in heaven. When he sees half-dead him whom none could cure before . . . he came near him.[15]

In other words, the Samaritan is an allegorical representation of Jesus, the only one who can save and who is better than all who came before.

---

12. Green, *Gospel of Luke*, 429. See also Levine, *Short Stories by Jesus*, 92.
13. Green, *Gospel of Luke*, 429.
14. See the perspectives documented in Levine, *Short Stories by Jesus*, 99–100.
15. Just, *Ancient Christian Commentary*, 179–80. See also Roukema, "Good Samaritan," 56–74.

Within the story, Luke gives no information about the motivations of the priest and the Levite. Were such motives pertinent, we might suppose he would have made them explicit. Their passing by is narrated with no detail. A. J. Levine turns to Martin Luther King Jr. to offer perhaps the best explanation of their motivation in not helping the man:

> I'm going to tell you what my imagination tells me. It's possible these men were afraid . . . And so the first question that the priest [and] the Levite asked was, "If I stop to help this man, what will happen to me?" But then the Good Samaritan came by, and he reversed the question: "If I do not stop to help this man, what will happen to him?"[16]

We do not need to reconstruct slanderous depictions of sanctimonious first-century Jews in order to understand Jesus's point. King gets it right: they were selfish and self-centered and cared not for the man half dead.

The part of the parable that focuses on the Samaritan has quite a bit more detail. We learn about his beast, his oil and wine, and his coinage. He is also a Samaritan. This is not the only place in the New Testament where Samaritans are mentioned. Jesus's long discussion with the woman at the well in John 4 is interlaced with fascinating dialogue about Jewish and Samaritan theology. There the woman is a sympathetic figure who dialogues with Jesus while his disciples are off buying food. Luke, however, seems less sympathetic. Only one chapter earlier, Luke shares a brief anecdote:

> When the days drew near for him to be taken up, he set his face to go to Jerusalem. And he sent messengers ahead of him. On their way they entered a village of the Samaritans to make ready for him; but they did not receive him, because his face was set toward Jerusalem. When his disciples James and John saw it, they said, "Lord, do you want us to command fire to come down from heaven and consume them? But he turned and rebuked them. Then they went on to another village. (Luke 9:54–56)

The rejection here by the Samaritans "because his face was set towards Jerusalem" probably reflects the long-running dispute between Jews and Samaritans over the proper place for worship. Whatever the reason, this episode presents the enmity between the two groups rather harshly, especially in the disciples' proposed response. Their call for fire and brimstone hardly seems proportional to the rejection they had received, and Jesus

---

16. As quoted in Levine, *Short Stories by Jesus*, 102.

rightly rebukes them for it. With this story fresh in the reader's mind, it makes the disposition of this one particular Samaritan in the parable all the more unlikely and surprising.

The tension between Jews and Samaritans in the ancient world is not like the jokes that people in Minnesota tell about Iowans, (or Iowans, needing someone to pick on, tell about people in North Dakota). A better analogy would be the hostility between Shia and Sunni Muslims. They share a long history, but trace their origins to different patriarchal leaders. Such closeness can often breed new levels of hatred and resentment. One way to put this into perspective would be this: whom would you be least likely to help? Or, from whom would you be embarrassed or insulted to receive help? Some people fear and dislike Muslims in the modern day United States. If your stereotypical gun-toting, anti-immigration American ended up in the ditch and was passed by a Baptist pastor and a US congressperson, only to be helped by a wealthy Muslim refugee, then we might begin to comprehend the picture Luke was trying to paint.

The other key detail about this Samaritan is how he is moved to pity (10:33). The Greek word used to describe his emotional state refers to bowels or innards. It conveys the idea of being moved from within with compassion. Luke uses this word a few other places, usually to refer to Jesus having compassion on another. He also uses it to describe the emotion of the father in the parable of the prodigal son. When the father sees his son returning home from far off, he was moved with compassion for him. This compassion is linked with action. The characters in Luke's Gospel who exemplify mercy act on behalf of others.

After the story wraps up, with the Samaritan putting money on the table and committing to future outlays as well, Jesus turns back to the lawyer: "Which of these three, do you think, was a neighbor to the man who fell into the hands of the robbers?" The question hardly needed to be asked, but it does give the lawyer a chance to respond: "The one who showed him mercy." This is the first time that the word "mercy" has been used throughout the story. It suggests, first of all, that the lawyer understands mercy as basically synonymous with the language in verse 33, in which the Samaritan was moved in his innards with pity. Mercy, as a conclusion to this parable, is a welling up of emotion from deep within. It also helps us understand that mercy, in Luke's understanding of it, is not only emotional, but also requires action. In the conclusion to her study of this parable, A. J. Levine highlights the change from compassion to mercy in the concluding two verses:

The parable spoke about compassion, but the lawyer read the action as one of mercy. His rephrasing the issue is apt: compassion can be felt in the gut; mercy needs to be enacted with the body.[17]

Levine goes on to point out that, in other places in Luke, the word mercy tends to be used as an "attribute of the divine."[18] Luke uses this word particularly in his infancy narrative, where mercy is something that God provides. For example, God enacts mercy in 1:50 ("His mercy is for those who fear him") and in 1:72 ("thus he has shown the mercy promised to our ancestors"). Also, in the song of Zechariah, he refers to the "tender mercy of our God" which will break forth like the dawn (1:78).

Luke's Understanding of Mercy

How you understand Luke's view of mercy depends on how you read the parable. Ought we see ourselves as the random person in the ditch, or as the Samaritan who acts with mercy?

Although it may be legitimate to think of ourselves as the man in the ditch, I would suggest that the details of Luke's parable suggest otherwise. Luke has a penchant for leaving his stories and parables unfinished. The arc of certain characters is often not completed, leaving an open ending. For example, in the famous "Parable of the Prodigal Son" (15:11–32), the story ends with the father speaking to the older son, who is disgruntled at the lavish reception his brother has received after wasting his inheritance. They had to celebrate, the father explains, because his brother "was lost and has been found" (15:32). This statement ends the story, and we never know how the older brother responds. His character's arc is not finished.

In the story of the rich ruler (18:18–25), Luke has the story end similarly. Jesus tells the man that he must sell all of his possessions and give them to the poor. When the ruler hears this, "he became sad; for he was very rich" (18:23). This ends the rich ruler's story. We don't know how he responded. Is he sad because he is rich, will not change his ways, and therefore he will not make it to eternal life? Or is he sad because he is planning to give away all his possessions?

In both of these stories, Luke intentionally leaves the ending open. In the good Samaritan parable, the character whose story does not conclude

---

17. Levine, *Short Stories by Jesus*, 113–14.
18. Levine, *Short Stories by Jesus*, 114.

might give us some indication as to which character Luke is most interested in and point at why he was telling this story in the first place. We have no worries about the man who was beaten; he's been taken care of. The Samaritan, likewise, is not someone about whom we would have more questions. The story that frames the parable, however, is where Luke draws our attention. Here Luke has Jesus point directly at the Samaritan as the key figure in the story. The Samaritan is the one doing the mercy, and he is the one whom Jesus says to emulate. I would suggest that to read this story as if we are all lying in a ditch waiting to experience God's mercy would not be the best reading. A better reading would suggest that we ought to put ourselves in the shoes of the lawyer, and therefore the Samaritan, in how we interpret the parable.

If we read the story in order to emulate the Samaritan, it becomes a call to act with mercy. This becomes difficult when we realize that mercy is extended lavishly on those whom we would consider our enemies. Can we enact what Jesus said the lawyer must do? This is the call that Pope Francis sees when he reads many different stories from Scripture: "The mercy of God is his loving concern for each one of us. He feels responsible; that is, he desires our wellbeing and he wants to see us happy, full of joy, and peaceful. This is the path which the merciful love of Christians must also travel. As the Father loves, so do his children. Just as he is merciful, so we are called to be merciful to each other."[19]

Conclusion

In his "Bull of Indiction" introducing the year of mercy, Pope Francis provides an overview of how he thinks about the idea of mercy. This document, titled *Misericordiae Vultus*, is infused with reflections on Scripture. He focuses at one point on the parable of the "Ruthless Servant" from Matthew 18. In this parable, which may stand out for you if you know the musical *Godspell*, a king decides to settle accounts with his slaves. One owed the king "ten thousand talents" (Matt 18:24). A talent was worth a large sum of money in the ancient world, somewhere between six and ten thousand denarii (a denarius was the usual one-day pay for a laborer). So, ten thousand talents was an incredibly large sum of money. *Godspell's* claim, that his debt ran into the millions, isn't quite drastic enough. Today it would be like the phrase "a billion dollars," an unimaginable sum. One wonders what a slave

---

19. Francis, *Misericordiae Vultus*, 9.

could have done to be so deeply in debt. The number is meant to be astronomical to help drive home the point of the parable. The king was moved to pity for the man (the same Greek word used in Luke's parable to describe the action of the good Samaritan) and forgives his entire debt.

As the parable continues, someone approaches the man whose debts were forgiven, also asking for debt forgiveness. This time the debt is one hundred denarii. This is still a substantial sum (not the two dollars in the *Godspell* version), but a fraction of what this man had owed to the king. Indifferent to how he had been treated, he throws the man owing one hundred denarii into prison until he could pay the debt. It doesn't take long for news of this callous action to make it back to the king, who becomes irate: "You wicked slave! I forgave you all that debt because you pleaded with me. Should you not have had mercy on your fellow slave, as I had mercy on you?" (Matt 18:32–33).

In his interpretation of this parable, Pope Francis comes to a very similar conclusion to that which we explored in the good Samaritan story: "Jesus affirms that mercy is not only an action of the Father, it becomes a criterion for ascertaining who his true children are. In short, we are called to show mercy because mercy has first been shown to us." For Francis, being merciful "is an imperative from which we cannot excuse ourselves."[20]

As we can see, mercy is certainly a worthwhile concept to explore within Scripture. Pope Francis's exploration of this word and concept is steeped in Scripture, even if the specifics are not always relayed in that exact way. Although the roots are deep, Archbishop Donald Bolen claims that there is something new here as well: "a new emphasis, a creative and strong proclamation of mercy that resounds from [Francis's] pontificate. One gets the sense that he would be stumbling for words without it, and at the same time he loads it with meaning as vast and comprehensive as God's relationship with humanity."[21]

For Pope Francis, and in Scripture in general, there is at times an emphasis on personal mercy. In other words, there are times where it might be appropriate to think of ourselves as the ones who are half dead in the ditch. In the Psalms, this comes to the forefront. For example, Psalm 103 describes God as forgiving "all your iniquity" and crowning "you with steadfast mercy" (Ps 103:3–4). Francis is keen on emphasizing that God's mercy is showered upon a broken human situation. God never tires of forgiving.

20. Francis, *Misericordiae Vultus*, 9.
21. Bolen, "Mercy," 128.

As Bolen says, "mercy is the shape God's love takes when responding to human beings."[22] This means that mercy is more than just an "abstract idea, but a concrete reality."[23] Francis describes this mercy as a "visceral love" that "gushes forth from the depths naturally."[24] A visceral love that gushes forth might nicely encapsulate the way we saw the connection between pity and mercy in the parables from Luke and Matthew, explored above.

Even in the Psalms, however, Francis pivots to mention those on whom God's mercy is poured out, particularly the poor, the oppressed, and the hungry (e.g., Ps 146:7–9). Here we find the most challenging aspect of God's mercy, mentioned briefly before: God's mercy is not always directed at "us." Most people living in the modern day United States do not qualify as the oppressed, hungry, prisoner, or bowed down, those singled out by Psalm 146 and by Pope Francis as those who are the primary recipients of God's mercy. Francis, for example, claims that God shows the poor "his first mercy."[25] This may not seem fair, but it is a clear component of how Scripture talks about mercy, and is doubtless the main way that Pope Francis thinks about it as well. God's mercy is not equally shed on all humans, but is predisposed toward the poor, the suffering, and the oppressed.

If mercy is primarily directed at the "other," then it is incumbent upon individuals and the church to bring God's mercy to others. In both the parable of the good Samaritan and the ruthless ruler, mercy required specific action. Francis claims that the church can be "authentic and credible only when [it] becomes a convincing herald of mercy." This is its "task."[26] His entire ministry as a priest had been focused on the poor and the outcast, and his emphasis on mercy amounts to what we might call a new ecclesiology, a "model of Church."[27] Mercy, Francis claims, can never be an abstraction: "By its very nature, it indicates something concrete: intentions, attitudes, and behaviors that are shown in daily living."[28]

---

22. Bolen, "Mercy," 129.
23. Francis, *Misericordiae Vultus*, 6.
24. Francis, *Misericordiae Vultus*, 6.
25. Francis, *Evangelii Gaudium*, 198.
26. Francis, *Misericordiae Vultus*, 25.
27. Ivereigh, *Great Reformer*, 220.
28. Francis, *Misericordiae Vultus*, 9.

7

Francis's Disdain: Rigid Adherence to Law

The church is not a tollhouse.[1]

IN THE ACTS OF the Apostles, Philip baptizes a God-curious eunuch from Ethiopia (8:26–40). An angel of God tells Philip to go south to the "wilderness road" between Jerusalem and Gaza (8:26), where Philip encounters an official from the court of the queen of the Ethiopians. This eunuch had been to Jerusalem to worship, and he was reading the prophet Isaiah on his way back. Philip starts with a question: "do you understand what you are reading?" (8:30). The eunuch replies that he could not understand without someone to guide him. After Philip explains the passage in Isaiah, the eunuch asks his own question: "Look, here is water! What is to prevent me from being baptized?" Philip answers with action, not words. They get out of the chariot and Philip baptizes him.

On May 8, 2014, Pope Francis delivered a homily in which he focused on this reading in Acts 8. He used the story as a chance to reflect on how we "facilitate the sacraments."[2] Francis points out in the story how Philip started with a question, not a statement or creed. Philip is ready to share the gospel, but he starts a conversation, which Francis claims is a requirement. Francis also points out how Philip erects no impediments to the eunuch in his desire for baptism. The homily continues with a longer reflection on how the church has to be "trusting in grace" because "grace is more important than any bureaucracy."[3] He ends by saying, "so often

---

1. Francis, *Evangelii Gaudium*, 47.
2. Francis, *Morning Homilies III*, 118.
3. Francis, *Morning Homilies III*, 121.

we in the church become a business creating impediments to keep people from coming to grace."[4]

Pope Francis's interpretation of this story is a leading indicator of how he sees many things. One of the major themes of his ministry, something to which he returns time and again, is the problem of church rules that get in the way of people's experience of God's grace. Impediments to God's grace run the risk of limiting God's movement in the church among the people. He says in *Evangelii Gaudium* that the gospel has to be expressed in ever new forms and language. He also alludes to Thomas Aquinas when he says that Jesus gave very few direct commands. Jesus was, generally speaking, not a rule-giver (there are obvious exceptions). This leads Francis to claim that "too many rules can become a form of servitude for the religion."[5]

Such language might understandably make some people nervous. The Roman Catholic Church has been known for its rules and rigor. Francis admits as much, acknowledging that an ever-flowering understanding of the gospel might lead to confusion or be undesirable "for those who long for a monolithic body of doctrine guarded by all and leaving no room for nuance." But, he says, "in fact such variety serves to bring out and develop different facets of the inexhaustible riches of the Gospel."[6]

What one finds in Scripture is a very similar tension between the rules and regulations of religious traditions and an open and less rule-bound understanding of God's action. In this chapter, we will try to get a sense of some of these tensions, where they come from, and how the biblical authors dealt with them and why. We will start with two texts in the Old Testament, the books of Amos and Micah, which offer critiques of some religious practice of their day. Then, we will explore these tensions in the Gospel of Matthew and look at one of Francis's favorite topics: the Pharisees.

Throughout this chapter, we must be very careful. One of the traditional ways Christianity has been understood is that Jesus came and rescued humanity from the rigorous and legalistic laws of Judaism. Nothing could be farther from the truth. We find plenty of self-critique within ancient Judaism itself, and there are many rules and regulations set up within early Christianity. Nevertheless, an unfortunate stereotype, one perpetuated by the New Testament itself and countless church leaders across the centuries, has often led to severe violence against the Jewish people. The problem of

---

4. Francis, *Morning Homilies III*, 121.
5. Francis, *Evangelii Gaudium*, 43.
6. Francis, *Evangelii Gaudium*, 40.

anti-Semitism is one against which we must be vigilant, and we will address it at several points throughout this chapter.

Micah and Amos—Intra-Jewish Critique

Our discussion of prophets in the Old Testament will focus on those who hail from the eighth century BCE. At this time period, we see some of the prophets of ancient Israel critiquing those who thoughtlessly adhere to the rules while ignoring other tenets of the people's relationship with God. The authors of the New Testament pick up these same themes as well.

Amos

As we noted in an earlier chapter when discussing Amos, this prophetic book was written at a time of general prosperity and tranquility for the northern kingdom of Israel. Our focus in chapter 3 was on Amos's call for social justice. Here we will observe more broadly how that justice relates to the religious practices of the eighth century BCE. The people who were profiting from the economic system wanted their religious festivals to be over quickly because economic activity would stop during the festivals. Amos quotes the leaders as asking: "when will the new moon be over so that we may sell grain; and the Sabbath, so that we may offer wheat for sale?" (Amos 8:5). In other words, "when will this holiday be over so we can get back to making money?" In addition, Amos accuses the leaders of using tricked scales and unfair balances to filch money from the poor and those who depend upon their leadership. These leaders were not eschewing the technical observances of their religion. They "kept" the Sabbath, "observed" festivals, and were "singing" their worship songs. The problem, according to Amos, is that they were missing something else: mercy and justice.

In chapter 7, God shows Amos a plumb line, typically used in construction to make certain that walls were vertically straight. The text says that God will set a plumb line among the people. Using such an image suggests that the people have built improperly, that their actions were askew. Because of this,

> The high places of Isaac shall be made desolate,
> and the sanctuaries of Israel shall be laid waste. (Amos 7:9)

God will destroy their places of worship. The songs that they sing in worship will be turned into a wail (8:3). Amos goes so far as to hint that the punishment for their lack of mercy and justice will resemble that which God brought on Egypt: the Nile will rise, the sun will go down at noon, sackcloth will be worn by all, and mourning will be like that for the loss of an only child (8:9–10). God's word will be removed from them (8:11–12).

The point of all of this is not just that God requires justice in the social realm (as we saw in chapter 3), but that the observance of their religion can't save them. Keeping the feasts and Sabbaths is not enough. Erecting shrines in holy places is not enough. There is, for the prophet Amos, a more basic requirement of mercy that has not been established. Amos's agenda is a self-critique within the Hebrew Scriptures and ancient Israelite society. The traditions of Israel were far from monolithic, and one of the roles of the prophets in the ancient world was to critique their society and their religious practice. Their songs and observances would not shield them from the broad demands of God.

Pope Francis discusses this very tension, although he gets there through a different set of daily readings, in a homily from Monday, December 16, 2013. He utilizes the role of prophecy, noting how all Christians are baptized as prophets. A prophet, he claims, interacts with past, present, and future. At times when there is not a sufficient prophetic voice, a "legalism steps in."[7] Some people who lose sight of the broader aims of God can be "unable to read the signs of the time; they didn't have clear eyes and were unable to hear the word of God. All they had was authority."[8] This might describe the situation behind the book of Amos rather well. There are people in charge, but all that matters to them is what is "present" and what is "legal." To use Francis's language to explain Amos, we might say that those running the religion and the economic system were concerned with technical observances. The prophet Amos demolishes this viewpoint from within the tradition. He remembers God's judgment from the past, he condemns the lack of mercy in the present, and he calls for a future in which there will be a dramatic reversal.

---

7. Francis, *Morning Homilies II*, 144.
8. Francis, *Morning Homilies II*, 144.

Micah

Parts of the book of Micah give a prophetic critique similar to what we just explored in Amos. The introduction to the book of Micah gives us a brief sketch of this prophet:

> The word of the LORD that came to Micah of Moresheth in the days of Kings Jotham, Ahaz, and Hezekiah of Judah, which he saw concerning Samaria and Jerusalem. (Mic 1:1)

The kings named in this introduction place Micah in the second half of the eighth century BCE. This makes him a contemporary with Amos. Moresheth is a town about twenty miles outside of Jerusalem.

Micah's ministry as a prophet follows directly upon the relative flourishing during the time of Amos. Micah's ministry, however, spans a more serious militaristic threat from Assyria. Micah was not a man of the city or the king's court like his contemporary Isaiah. He was from the countryside, a prophet of the people. Micah 3 pronounces a devastating set of woes upon the leadership of his day. Micah has priests, prophets, and kings in his sights (3:11) because they have not been caring for the people properly. Micah uses an image of consumption: the leaders are flaying the skin off of God's people and eating them:

> Listen, you heads of Jacob
>   And rulers of the house of Israel!
> Should you not know justice?—
>   You who hate the good and love the evil,
> Who tear the skin off my people,
>   And the flesh off their bones.
> who eat the flesh of my people,
>   flay their skin off them,
> break their bones in pieces,
>   and chop them up like meat in a kettle,
>   like flesh in a caldron. (Mic 3:1–3)

These words are a prophetic call for justice, very similar to what we saw in Amos. The imagery is quite graphic. Pope Francis, although not overtly citing it, was perhaps inspired by such language when describing the plight of the poor in our world today:

> Can we continue to stand by when food is thrown away while people are starving? This is a case of inequality. Today everything comes under the laws of competition and the survival of the fittest,

where the powerful feed upon the powerless ... Human beings are themselves considered consumer goods to be used and then discarded ... The excluded are not the "exploited" but the outcast, the "leftovers."[9]

Francis, like Micah, turns the people into food—fileted, consumed, or thrown away.

The prophet Micah takes this accusation one step further and suggests that the leaders who are oppressing the little people are doing so while hiding behind their religiosity. He quotes them as saying, "Surly the LORD is with us! No harm shall come upon us." In chapter 6, Micah makes this even more explicit. Micah asks what will make God happy, what shall people bring before the LORD?

> With what shall I come before the LORD,
>   and bow myself before God on high?
> Shall I come before him with burnt offerings,
>   with calves a year old?
> Will the LORD be pleased with thousands of rams,
>   with ten thousands of rivers of oil?
> Shall I give my firstborn for my transgression,
>   the fruit of my body for the sin of my soul?"
> He has told you, O mortal, what is good;
>   And what does the LORD require of you
> but to do justice, and to love kindness,
>   and to walk humbly with your God? (Mic 6:6–8)

Micah claims that the regular trappings of religious observance cannot move God if the people are missing a more fundamental sense of justice. Sacrifices of food, oil, animals, or even humans will never be sufficient if people do not live with a basic sense of justice and humility. There must be a correspondence between act and intention, between the inside and the outside. Not even a river of oil, offered as a sacrifice to God, will make God happy if more basic requirements are not met.

The preceding discussion is important for two reasons. First, it highlights the fact that there was plenty of self-critique within the Jewish tradition. This sets the table for a second important conclusion: when we find critique of Jewish traditions or ideas within the New Testament, we are not seeing a "Christian" critique of "Judaism," but an intra-Jewish discussion that continues what had already been ongoing for centuries: a Judaism that

---

9. Francis, *Evangelii Gaudium*, 53.

was diverse and struggled with questions of what is essential in God's eyes and how to make sense of God in changing world situations.

The New Testament

If we turn to the New Testament, we see some of the same tensions as in Amos and Micah. In the Gospels, Jesus often dons a prophetic mantle and offers critiques of the Jewish leadership of his time period. While this tension can be observed in many parts of the New Testament, we will focus here initially on the Gospel of Matthew. We must remember that the Gospels are not primarily historical documents. We have four of them because they are each different, giving us slightly different depictions and interpretations of the life of Jesus. They are more like homilies or icons, meant to inspire, inform, and move people to action. They are not newspaper articles written with a journalistic interest in "what happened." Our goal here will be to understand the particular depiction of Jesus in Matthew's Gospel and how it relates to our broader topic of religious observance in continuity with the Old Testament.

Matthew

The Gospel of Matthew was probably written toward the end of the first century, some fifty-five to sixty-five years after Jesus's death and resurrection. Many of the ways Matthew depicts Jesus, such as his childhood flight to Egypt and giving of the law from a mountaintop, make Jesus reminiscent of Moses. Scholars refer to Jesus in Matthew's Gospel as a "new Moses." Within this framework, the specific ways that Matthew depicts Jesus's giving of the law is one that stretches, reinterprets, or redefines previous understandings. We must remember that "Christianity" as a religion doesn't exist yet. Matthew understood himself as within the Jewish tradition. Following Matthew's version of the Beatitudes, for example, Jesus reinterprets the Ten Commandments and other well-known Jewish laws of the day:

> You have heard that it was said to those of ancient times, "you shall not murder" ... but I say to you that if you are angry with a brother or sister, you will be liable to judgment. (Matt 5:21–22)

Such reinterpretations continue for issues related to adultery and lust, lawsuits, oath-making, and violence. In other words, Matthew seems interested in presenting Jesus as the one who can authoritatively reinterpret his Jewish traditions for a new generation of believers.

At several points, this reinterpretation takes the form of a prophetic critique quite similar to what we saw in Amos and Micah. One example comes in the midst of a chain of stories in chapter 9:

> As Jesus was walking along, he saw a man called Matthew sitting at the tax booth; and he said to him, "Follow me." And he got up and followed him.
>
> And as he sat at dinner in the house, many tax collectors and sinners came and were sitting with him and his disciples. When the Pharisees saw this, they said to his disciples, "Why does your teacher eat with tax collectors and sinners?" But when he heard this, he said, "Those who are well have no need of a physician, but those who are sick. Go and learn what this means, 'I desire mercy, not sacrifice.' For I have come to call not the righteous but sinners." (Matt 9:9–13)

The quotation at the end of this episode comes from the book of Hosea in the Old Testament. Hosea was from the same century as Amos and Micah, although his critique focused more on idolatry than on social justice. Nevertheless, he hews close to the same idea of what is essential in God's eyes when he quotes God as saying:

> For I desire steadfast love and not sacrifice,
>   the knowledge of God rather than burnt offerings. (Hos 6:6)

Matthew's appropriation of this quote exemplifies one of the recurring themes of his Gospel: Jesus's apparent disregard for the regulations of the law as they had come to be understood by certain Jewish leaders, particularly the Pharisees. Jesus shows no regard for such laws. Jesus instead tells the Pharisees to go and learn what the saying from Hosea means, although he gives no practical advice as to how they were supposed to do that. Jesus infers that living by his example would enact Hosea's vision.

After this story, Jesus offers a brief teaching to his disciples that specifically engages in language of old and new:

> No one sews a piece of unshrunk cloth on an old cloak, for the patch pulls away from the cloak, and a worse tear is made. Neither is new wine put into old wineskins; otherwise, the skins burst, and the wine is spilled, and the skins are destroyed; but new wine is put into fresh wineskins, and so both are preserved. (Matt 9:16–17)

While such language has given rise to negative attitudes from Christians toward Jews, Matthew asks his readers to think about a calcified tradition and the need for newness. Matthew culls this idea from the Old Testament and applies it across the face of Jesus's ministry.

A couple of chapters later, Matthew quotes the same verse from Hosea in a context that is similar to the first. In this story, the question is not of eating with sinners, but the fact that Jesus and his disciples were plucking heads of grain and eating them on the Sabbath. This, presumably, would have broken the command not to work on the Sabbath. The Pharisees see this and question Jesus about it. Jesus turns to the Old Testament for an explanation:

> Have you not read what David did when he and his companions were hungry? He entered the house of God and ate the bread of the Presence, which it was not lawful for him or his companions to eat, but only for the priests . . . But if you had known what this means, "I desire mercy and not sacrifice," you would not have condemned the guiltless. For the Son of Man is lord of the sabbath. (Matt 12:3–8)

The point here recapitulates the one from chapter 9, that a life with God requires something different than just adherence to rules. The Sabbath rules mean nothing if there is a crisis, if people are hungry, or there is an emergency. In the next section, Jesus asks: "Suppose one of you has only one sheep and it falls into a pit on the sabbath; will you not lay hold of it and lift it out? . . . So it is lawful to do good on the sabbath" (Matt 12:11–12). Matthew's point is to show that a strict adherence to law is not a good thing, that the whole situation must be considered.

This very dynamic is one that Pope Francis often points to in the church today. In *Evangelii Gaudium* he talks about how churches often make an unwelcoming atmosphere, and that we often find a "bureaucratic way of dealing with problems, be they simple or complex, in the lives of our people. In many places an administrative approach prevails over a pastoral approach."[10] In another place, his language is even stronger as he describes the "Promethean neo-Pelagianism of those who ultimately trust only in their own powers and feel superior to others because they observe certain rules or remain intransigently faithful to a particular Catholic style from

---

10. Francis, *Evangelii Gaudium*, 63.

the past. A supposed soundness of doctrine or discipline leads instead to a narcissistic and authoritarian elitism."[11]

These are tough words from Pope Francis when applied to our world and our churches today. Critics who have found his language and ministry to be insufficiently focused on clarity of doctrine have not always met such language with alacrity. But Francis sees a problem in the way some priests close the door on people. He tells stories of parents not allowed to attend their child's baptism because of divorce or other factors.[12] These types of stories are typical of the homespun anecdotes of which Francis is quite fond. Francis's emphasis emerges from key dynamics of the biblical text. Parts of the Old Testament, and much of the New Testament, testify to the ongoing struggle of how to integrate newness with adherence to religious traditions. When a prophetic leader (like Amos, Jesus, or Pope Francis) wants to push a religious tradition in new directions, there are bound to be those who will object. The objection tends to be that "this is not how we do things" or "this is not how we've ever done things."

On April 27, 2017, Pope Francis addressed a group known as Catholic Action, a lay movement started in Europe in the 1800s. In his address to this group, Francis said that we must never use the phrase "It's always been done this way," calling this phrase "bad."[13] He continues: "The 'always done this way' phrase has done so much damage in the Church, and it continues to do so much damage to the Church . . . We must always be changing because time changes. The only thing that does not change is what's essential. What doesn't change is the announcement of Jesus Christ, missionary attitude, prayer, the need to pray, the need to be formed, and the need to sacrifice."[14]

One image Francis has used in such discussions is that of an anchor. This is a subtle evocation of the metaphor of a boat that has been used for the church across the centuries. In early Christian art, Noah's ark was used as a metaphor for the church, an enclave of God's safety and guidance in a stormy world. Early Christians also used an anchor as a symbol of strength and hope, perhaps inspired by Hebrews 6:19, which describes hope as an anchor for the soul. Francis insists that the church must be anchored to a future hope, one that is not entirely knowable. We are drawn along the rope connected to this anchor. But, Francis asks, where are we really anchored?

11. Francis, *Evangelii Gaudium*, 94
12. Glatz, "Pope Francis," para. 7.
13. Mickens, "Don't Say," paras. 28–30.
14. Mickens, "Don't Say," paras 31–32.

"Are we anchored in an artificial pond made by ourselves, with our own rules, our own activities, our own timetables, our own clericalism and ecclesiastical attitudes—and we don't mean the mind of the church. Are we anchored there where everything is safe and comfy?"[15]

These words are Pope Francis's attempt to read the gospel in light of our modern situation. He seems particularly concerned with the ways in which the structures of the church—often couched as clericalism or excessive legalism—might impede a more pastoral approach, one more in tune with the spirit of the moment. His reflections and warnings have deep biblical roots.

The Pharisees

Pope Francis often refers to people or groups within the church today as Pharisees. For example, in the speech given to the Catholic Action group we discussed above, he pivots from his discussion of the changing times to Matthew 23, which is a long screed against the scribes and Pharisees in which Jesus calls these leaders "hypocrites." For Francis, the Pharisees are those in the church today who want to "regulate things and not allow freedom."[16]

As previously mentioned, during a daily homily, Francis told the following anecdote and left no doubt that he sees the dynamics of the Pharisees still in the church today:

> Three months ago, in a country, in a city, a mother wanted to baptize her newly born son, but she was married civilly to a divorced man. The priest said, "Yes, yes. Baptize the baby. But your husband is divorced, so he cannot be present at the ceremony." This is happening today. The Pharisees, or Doctors of the Law, are not people of the past, even today there are many of them.[17]

Such language from the pope might warrant us asking who the Pharisees were. Were they really such bad people? And is Pope Francis justified in referring to church members today by this title? This language is common enough from Francis that we should stop and consider who the Pharisees were and how they are depicted in the Gospels, in order to understand how and why Francis is so fond of them as a metaphor.

---

15. Francis, *Morning Homilies II*, 86.
16. Mickens, "Don't Say," para. 33.
17. "Pope at Santa Marta," 0:15–1:02.

The New Testament usually presents the Pharisees as sticklers for the rules, that they have malice in their hearts, and that they attempted to ensnare Jesus at every turn. This depiction is a caricature. Our knowledge of the Pharisees in the ancient world is far from perfect, but there are some things that we can learn about them historically.

The Pharisees of History

Judaism in the first century was diverse. There were many different groups and ideologies within it. Although all Jews shared much in common, such as their Scriptures, the temple, and the legacy of their ancestors and laws, they disagreed on a number of fundamental issues. For example, some Jews in the first century believed in an afterlife and a future resurrection, while some rejected such ideas outright. Groups also disagreed on how to interpret their Scriptures. The New Testament discusses some of these groups, such as the Pharisees, Sadducees, Herodians, scribes, and chief priests. Ancient sources tell us about other groups as well, such as the Essenes, an ascetic group that may have connections to the group that wrote the Dead Sea Scrolls. Judaism was not monolithic; it had a variety of groups, ideologies, and approaches to their faith. The Pharisees were one identifiable historical group within this diversity.

The Pharisees' origin stretches back into the second century BCE. They had distinct and innovative beliefs for this time period. Outside of the New Testament, one of the main places we learn about the Pharisees is from a Jewish historian named Josephus. He lived in the first century and provides direct information about the traditions of Judaism in the time of Jesus and the New Testament (although he does not refer to Jesus or Christians at any point in his writings). Josephus says that there were about six thousand Pharisees.[18] They based their work in the synagogue, a gathering place for Jewish worship especially important for Jews who did not live in close vicinity to the temple in Jerusalem. This means that the Pharisees led local communities scattered throughout the ancient world; their power was not primarily based in Jerusalem. They also do not seem to be from any priestly lineage associated with the temple or its workings.

From what Josephus says, the Pharisees were known for their interpretation of the Jewish law: "the Pharisees had passed on to the people certain regulations handed down by former generations and not recorded

18. Josephus, *Ant.* 17.42.

in the Laws of Moses."[19] This provides evidence that the Pharisees had a tradition of oral interpretation of the law that was passed down through authoritative teachers or rabbis. They did not just stick to the laws as written in the Torah. For the Pharisees, the law was flexible, in the sense that it could be subject to ongoing oral interpretation, or reinterpretation, in light of new situations. Groups like the Sadducees were much more conservative on this question, arguing that Jews should stick to what is written in the law itself and not attempt new interpretations. In fact, Josephus notes the animosity between Pharisees and Sadducees over how to interpret the law: "and concerning these matters the two parties came to have controversies and serious differences."[20] The Pharisees were the liberals of their day, embracing oral interpretations of the law and new and innovative theological ideas, such as the afterlife and resurrection (things that were not traditionally a part of the Jewish belief throughout their history).

Scholars also use sociological models to help us understand the role of the Pharisees in the ancient world. While such work is always conjectural, it can help us move beyond a definition of the Pharisees tied only to their specific beliefs. Anthony Saldarini has provided the most thorough sociological analysis of the Pharisees. He concludes that they were a political interest group. They had goals for society and engaged in political activities to achieve those goals. They were a highly literate voluntary organization that constantly sought influence with the ruling class. In sociological terms, they belong in what is called the "retainer" class, "a group of people above the peasants and other lower classes but dependent on the governing class and ruler for their place in society."[21] Being a Pharisee was not the only component of one's identity in the ancient world. Familial ties and identity remained strong, as did the need for a profession and other civic duties.[22]

The Pharisees found themselves, like any number of ancient groups, with a particular view of the world, and they worked at every opportunity to inculcate that view in society. Also like other groups, "when the opportunity arose, they sought power over society."[23] The New Testament depiction of them as hypocrites likely has little basis in reality. As Frederick Murphy has pointed out, "it stretches the imagination to think that the thousands

19. Josephus, *Ant.* 13.297.
20. Josephus, *Ant.* 13.297.
21. Saldarini, *Pharisees*, 281.
22. Saldarini, *Pharisees*, 284.
23. Saldarini, *Pharisees*, 284.

of members of a group whose difficult goal was to implement the Torah in their daily lives were each and every one of them hypocrites."[24]

The Pharisees of the New Testament

What does the New Testament actually say about Pharisees, and does it align with what history tells us about them? The first data point would be the Apostle Paul's claim to be a Pharisee. Paul, in a context in which he is bragging about his Jewish heritage, says, "if anyone else has reason to be confident in the flesh, I have more: circumcised on the eighth day, a member of the people of Israel, of the tribe of Benjamin, a Hebrew born of Hebrews; as to the law, a Pharisee; as to zeal, a persecutor of the church; as to righteousness under the law, blameless" (Phil 3:4–6). This is the only time Paul mentions this fact in his letters, but it does situate us to make some broad observations. First, there was some ideological overlap between early Christians and the Pharisees; they had similar theological viewpoints. For instance, both groups had a strong belief in an afterlife and resurrection. Christians obviously understood this differently given their belief that Jesus had already been resurrected, but the broad contours of belief are similar. Second, Paul provides evidence of a Pharisee's training in the ancient world. He was well-educated, fluent in Greek forms of communication and rhetoric, and fused those with an intimate knowledge of the Jewish Scriptures and their interpretation.

Other than Paul's use of the word in Philippians, the Pharisees only appear in the New Testament in the Gospels and in the Acts of the Apostles. These stories evince some accuracy regarding the Pharisees. Our earliest Gospel, Mark, relates a story in which the Pharisees are puzzled about how Jesus and his disciples do not follow guidelines of ritual purity. Mark recounts some of the practices typical for Pharisees: hand-washing and the washing of pots and cups before eating. Because of all of this, the Pharisees ask Jesus, "Why do your disciples not live according to the tradition of the elders?" (Mark 7:5). This information about the Pharisees fits well with what we might know of them from other sources: they had a long tradition of following rules passed down according to a certain tradition. Although Jesus does here call the Pharisees hypocrites, Mark does not attribute to them the same level of nefariousness as Matthew does.

---

24. Murphy, *Religious World of Jesus*, 221.

FRANCIS'S DISDAIN: RIGID ADHERENCE TO LAW

In 70 CE, the Romans destroyed the temple in Jerusalem, a cataclysmic event for the ancient Jews. The change this brought would have been particularly drastic for the Jewish leadership in Jerusalem. The war with Rome and the temple's destruction created a power vacuum for the varied landscape of Judaism in the first century. Both Pharisees and early Christians attempted to fill this vacuum. Because of the overlap in their beliefs that we have already explored, it would make sense that, in the rush to fill this power vacuum, Christians and Pharisees would have come into increasingly brutal conflict toward the end of the first century, which is exactly what we see in the Gospel of Matthew. As one scholar has summarized the situation: "Matthew harbors special animosity towards the Pharisees."[25] We see this most clearly in Matthew 23, which blossoms into a full-scale screed against the Pharisees. In this discourse, Matthew's Jesus lays serious allegations against the Pharisees. The complaints are many:

- Jesus calls them hypocrites: "for they do not practice what they teach." (23:3). Jesus says they lay heavy burdens on others, but won't lift a finger themselves.

- Jesus says they are seekers of fame and honor, requesting the best places at banquets (23:6–7).

- Jesus calls them "blind guides" and "blind fools" (23:16–17) because they have lost sight of what is important, focusing instead on insignificant matters. Here Matthew uses the vivid accusation that they strain out a gnat while swallowing a camel (23:24).

- Matthew's Jesus also describes the Pharisees as being clean on the outside but dirty on the inside. Like a whitewashed tomb that might have a nice exterior, they are rotting on the inside.

- Finally, the Pharisees are accused of ignoring the more important matters of the law. In an echo of Hosea 6, and in line with what we saw earlier in Matthew 9 and 12, they have focused on minute matters (here represented as tithes involving spices) and ignored the more important matters of justice and mercy (23:23).

This is just a summary of the nasty, vicious language that is used in Matthew 23 about the Pharisees. As we have already seen, much of this is unfair to the Pharisees as we understand them as a historical group.

---

25. Murphy, *Religious World of Jesus*, 230.

The most important conflict between Christians and Pharisees was over the identity of Jesus and his role as Messiah. The key to understanding Matthew 23 is verses 8–10:

> But you are not to be called rabbi, for you have one teacher, and you are all students. And call no one your father on earth, for you have one Father—the one in heaven. Nor are you to be called instructors, for you have one instructor, the Messiah. (Matt 23:8–10)

Here, Matthew is putting Jesus, whom he calls the one, true, authoritative Rabbi, into conflict with all of those who would call themselves "rabbi" in the first century. The ascendant role of Jesus in the first century, as more than just a rabbi but as Messiah, obviates the need for anyone else to be a teacher. In the view of an early Christian like Matthew, there is now only one teacher and interpreter of the law: Jesus. For the Pharisees and their authoritative tradition of rabbis, such an idea would be abhorrent.

We must always remember that the terrible language used toward the Pharisees in the Gospel of Matthew (and elsewhere in the New Testament) is the result of a very specific situation in the ancient world. The conflict is akin to a domestic spat between relatives, not a debate between two world religions. It is a debate within Judaism itself, one with deep roots in its own history.

Pope Francis's Use of the Pharisees

If Pope Francis has any goal for the church, one of them seems to be to a desire to "make a mess."[26] His appropriation of the New Testament's language about Pharisees certainly accomplishes that, and in a way that may not always be helpful. In a homily from March 2015, Pope Francis read the story of the woman caught in adultery from John 8. He critiques those who brought the woman forward, saying "they thought they were pure because they observed the law . . . but they did not know mercy."[27] Such language seems to disregard the law completely, to undermine it, and runs the risk of anti-Semitism. Some Jewish rabbis in Rome are concerned that Francis's rhetoric contradicts what church teaching says about Jewish and Christian relationships:

---

26. Allen, *Francis Miracle*, 189.
27. "Pope," para. 2.

> What a shame that they [church teachings] should be contradicted on a daily basis by the homilies of the pontiff, who employs precisely the old, inveterate structure and its expressions, dissolving the contents of the aforementioned documents. One need think only of the law of "an eye for an eye" recently evoked by the Pope carelessly and mistakenly.[28]

It would be helpful if Francis would find a way to show some awareness of the historical situation of the early church and why it was in such conflict with the Jewish leadership. As Philip Cunningham has suggested,

> It is regrettable that Pope Francis does not occasionally mention the affinity between Jesus and his Pharisaic contemporaries or simply attribute to only some of the scribes or Pharisees the human temptation to sanctimoniousness or arrogance. Without such caveats, he risks unintentionally reinforcing Christian caricatures of Judaism.[29]

Cunningham also documents the very strong relationships Pope Francis has forged with Jewish leaders and communities throughout his ministry. Francis stopped to visit Jews in Philadelphia during his sojourn in the United States in 2015. He has also often spoken fondly of the revelation God gave through the Torah. So, while some of Francis's language may be problematic, calling him anti-Semitic is probably an unfair characterization. Cunningham concludes this way:

> It is clear that Pope Francis has great personal reverence for the Jewish people and tradition, for the Torah, and for the "journey of friendship" that Jews and Catholics have undertaken for more than fifty years. It is unfounded and unfair to accuse him of being "anti-Jewish" on the basis of a handful of ill-chosen comments intended as criticism of his own church.[30]

Conclusion

The challenge for the modern church, Pope Francis seems to be suggesting, is that the dynamic of old and new, of strict adherence with disregard for the Spirit, is not something that was isolated in the past. It was not only an

---

28. Palmieri-Billig, "Italy's Rabbis Protest," paras. 12–13.
29. Cunningham, "Is the Pope 'Anti-Jewish,'" para. 14.
30. Cunningham, "Is the Pope 'Anti-Jewish,'" para. 21.

issue in Jesus's day. This dynamic continues, and the "Pharisaic" mindset is a constant danger for the church.

Francis has a strong sense of the Spirit and its movement in our world today. Francis often sets this emphasis up against the law or rigid adherence to doctrinal practice. For example, he will often use language that refers to the "doctors of the law" who limit God's love and forgiveness.[31] The place where this has become most specific is in the interpretation of the pope's apostolic exhortation *Amoris Laetitia*, published in 2016 as a conclusion to the synod on the family. Within this exhortation, Pope Francis allows a penitential path for individuals who have been divorced and remarried to receive communion even if they have not received an annulment. He emphasizes "pastoral discernment" and the need for priests to "accompany" individuals.[32] He says that "a sincere reflection can strengthen trust in the mercy of God which is not denied anyone."[33]

There has been much resistance to Pope Francis's words on divorce and remarriage in *Amoris Laetitia*. Francis views such opposition as akin to the opposition the Pharisees presented to Jesus, marked by excessive legalism and adherence to law. Opposition to God's grace in favor of legalism is done at the expense of a pastoral approach, one that might focus not on law, but on forgiveness and mercy. Francis's basic vision was made clear in his first pastoral exhortation: "pastoral ministry in a missionary style is not obsessed with the disjointed transmission of a multitude of doctrines to be insistently imposed."[34]

Assessing Pope Francis's use of the Pharisees rests on answering a not-so-simple question: can the same dynamic that existed between the early church and some Pharisees explicate ongoing tensions within the church today? Can some parts of the magisterium of the church be in tension with its pastoral application and an emphasis on mercy? These questions are not easy to answer, but Pope Francis seems to think that the answer to each of them is "yes."

For better or worse, labeling people in the church today as "Pharisees" is one of Francis's calling cards. It may not always do justice to his opponents, for it turns them into an unfair caricature and decapitates any arguments in favor of a position with which Francis might disagree. It works

---

31. Wooden, "Do Not Be Fooled."
32. Francis, *Amoris Laetitia*, 300.
33. Francis, *Amoris Laetitia*, 300.
34. Francis, *Evangelii Gaudium*, 35.

instead in identity and paints the opposition as having a spiritual problem, which could undercut the very type of dialogue that Francis has tried to implement in the church.[35]

The tension between law and mercy that Francis sees in the church today is not new. It has deep roots in the Jewish tradition itself and is replete across the face of the New Testament. While Francis's rhetoric may occasionally go too far, we might do well to heed his concern. One of the core dynamics of the gospel that we have seen from Francis in other chapters of this book is how humans recoil when God's graciousness is bestowed on the "other." Mercy is just fine as long as it is showered up on us. Francis's insight here, at its very core, is about human reaction to God's graciousness and the fact that God might be more interested in helping someone other than you. Like the older brother in the parable of the prodigal son, how will we respond?

---

35. See Hillis, "Filled with Words of Love."

8

Francis's Journey: Uncertainty and Unanswered Questions

> When somebody has an answer for every question, it is a sign that they are not on the right road.[1]

How do we become certain of things? How do we know something is true? Our world is dominated by a scientific method of knowing, which involves observation, hypothesis, experiment, and verification. Some things can be proved experimentally and scientifically. I suspect that most people, however, do not live their lives in a scientifically calculated manner that leads to exactitude and certainty. We also have experiential ways of knowing that something is true. How, for instance, do you know that someone loves you, or that you love someone else? Love is not verifiable scientifically, but is grounded in emotion and experience, in hard work and example. Pablo Neruda captures this when he refers to holding on to a relationship with an aroma.[2] An aroma as a way of knowing something seems illogical, but might actually represent the emotional way of knowing with which most people live their lives.

This less verifiable, experiential, and relationship-based idea of knowing seems to infuse much of Pope Francis's ministry. His communication style—sprawling interviews and an informal, personal style—is indicative of his theological underpinnings: the life of faith is more journey and experience than it is writing everything down correctly. As Pope Francis says, "our life is not given to us like an opera libretto, in which all is written down; but

1. Francis, *Gaudete et Exsultate*, 41.
2. Neruda, *100 Love Sonnets*, 103.

it means going, walking, doing, searching, seeing."[3] This is the quest for God, one that, according to Francis, deals in approximations and must leave room for doubt, uncertainty, and unanswered questions.

Francis's theological formulations here, although not overtly based on the Bible, have deep resonances with many biblical formulations of the quest for God. God comes to us through Scripture in a wide variety of metaphor, analogy, and mystery. Furthermore, the Bible is the product of humans—inspired by God—but nevertheless written in human language and idioms, and, as a result, any language about God that we find in Scripture is tentative at best.

This chapter will examine the relationship between God and uncertainty by exploring three different texts. First, we will look at one of the most skeptical books in all of Scripture, Ecclesiastes, with an attempt to understand why its message is so skeptical and how we can make sense of it theologically today. Second, we turn to the New Testament and the story of the transfiguration in Mark's Gospel. The disciples want to enshrine a high point in the ministry of Jesus, but Jesus will not let them. Finally, we will discuss Paul's argument in Romans 9–11, in which he tackles the problem of Jews who do not believe in Jesus as Lord and Messiah. This causes him anguish and, ultimately, forces him to leave God and God's actions as a complete mystery.

Ecclesiastes

When I was a junior in college, I left the United States for the first time in order to study for a semester in Athens, Istanbul, and Rome. I was ignorant of what I would experience in other parts of the world. I grew up in a conservative Protestant church, and after two days in Athens my head was spinning because of how different Greek Orthodox Christianity was when compared to my own evangelical upbringing. One of my roommates was from a religious background similar to my own, and we decided to do a daily Bible study during the trip in order to keep ourselves grounded in our faith. For some reason, my friend chose Ecclesiastes as the biblical book we should start with. In the midst of personal upheaval, homesickness, and theological whiplash, we opened our Bibles and read the beginning of Ecclesiastes:

---

3. Spadaro, "Interview with Pope Francis," para. 80.

"Meaningless! Meaningless!" says the teacher. "Utterly meaningless! Everything is meaningless."[4] (Eccl 1:2)

My life has never been the same.

Everything is *Hevel*

The word that begins Ecclesiastes, translated above as "meaningless," is the Hebrew word *hevel*. This word evokes a puff of smoke or a vapor. Its connotations—something brief, fleeting, and indeterminate—are hard to convey in English. Translations use "vanity," "meaningless," or something similar. In the opening verses (1:4–11), the author attempts to prove that all is meaningless by contemplating the created order. The sun rockets around the earth (1:5). Streams flow to the sea, yet the sea does not fill (1:7). The wind blows around and around (1:6). In a prescientific world, none of these things can be explained, and their contemplation is "wearisome; more than one can express" (1:8). After reading this for a course, one of my students walked into class the next day and said, "that made me depressed." The author of Ecclesiastes does start to sound like Eeyore from the *Winnie the Pooh* books—morose, depressed, always looking at the negative side of things.

If one looks farther into the book, similar ideas continue to be pressed. In chapter 8, one finds a succinct summation of the book's perspective:

> There is a vanity that takes place on earth, that there are righteous people who are treated according to the conduct of the wicked, and there are wicked people who are treated according to the conduct of the righteous. I said that this is also vanity. So I commend enjoyment, for there is nothing better for people under the sun than to eat, and drink, and enjoy themselves. (8:14–15)

The author looks out at the world and sees that justice is not being enacted: wicked people are prospering and righteous people are suffering. Thus, all is *hevel*, meaninglessness or vanity. The same idea is repeated in the next chapter:

> Again I saw that under the sun the race is not to the swift, nor the battle to the strong, nor bread to the wise, nor riches to the intelligent, nor favor to the skillful; but time and chance happen to them all. For no one can anticipate the time of disaster. Like fish taken in

---

4. This is from the NIV translation, which I was reading at the time.

> a cruel net, and like birds caught in a snare, so mortals are snared
> at a time of calamity, when it suddenly falls upon them. (9:11–12)

One might read this and understandably come away depressed! It is a very skeptical interpretation of the world.

The core observation of Ecclesiastes has to do with "epistemology." This word refers to the study of what can be known. Thus, we can call the author of Ecclesiastes "epistemologically skeptical"; he or she seems reticent to say that humans can know anything at all. The time of calamity or how our lives will turn out are unknown to us, and not even being righteous can guarantee a secure future.

These observations explain why the author began with the word *hevel*. Life is fleeting. When examined closely, life seems like little more than a vapor or a puff of smoke. It lingers and then disappears. Life is also shapeless and unpredictable. It expands amorphously with no way of predicting where it will go.

Contextualizing Ecclesiastes's Skepticism

We might ask next: Why is Ecclesiastes so skeptical? There are two pieces of contextual information that will help illuminate the background of the epistemological viewpoint of Ecclesiastes.

Old Testament Context: Connection between Act and Consequence

First, Ecclesiastes sits in a theological context within the Old Testament itself. The book interacts with the theological idea that there is a close connection between action and consequence. For instance, in the book of Deuteronomy, we find a statement like this: "If you will only obey the Lord your God . . . all these blessings shall come upon you" (Deut 28:1–2). Deuteronomy states that the opposite is also true: "But if you will not obey the Lord your God . . . then all these curses shall come upon you" (Deut 28:15). This ideology, which suggests that God always treats humans according to their actions, has influenced large parts of the Old Testament. This close connection between act and consequence finds a particularly hospitable home in the wisdom literature in the Old Testament, especially the books of Proverbs and Sirach. Thus, Proverbs says, "Those who listen to me will be secure and will live at ease" (Prov 1:33). Sirach also has the same theological underpinning: "You who fear the Lord, trust in him, and your reward will not be lost" (Sir 2:8). Both of these texts are built on the same theological foundation from the book of Deuteronomy, that humans can know for certain how God will treat them because their destiny will be based on their righteousness.

Anyone should be able to see that such a tidy formula rarely works in reality. All it takes is a good person who gets cancer or a tsunami that indiscriminately kills hundreds of thousands of people to leave us in the same place as the author of Ecclesiastes: questioning the connection between righteousness and blessing. The formula as presented in Deuteronomy, Proverbs, and Sirach is too tidy and contradicted by life experience, which the author of Ecclesiastes bluntly points out: "the same fate comes to all, to the righteous and the wicked, to the good and the evil, to the clean and the unclean" (Eccl 9:2).

Historical Context: Economics

A second contextual piece of information illuminates Ecclesiastes, which has to do with its historical and economic context. While the book does not make any overt historical or chronological references, based on its language and ideas we can approximate its time and place. The evidence leads most scholars to date the book to the time when the Persians were in control of Judea (450–325 BCE). Under the Persians, taxation was widespread and highly organized. Coins were minted at unprecedented levels. The inscriptions from this period are preoccupied with economic matters.[5] Ecclesiastes displays a similar obsession with economic concerns. For example, after the opening reflection (Eccl 1:1–11), the author makes his observations concrete in the economic realm. Accumulated wealth and all of its trappings—houses, vineyards, herds, and silver—are nothing but a chasing after the wind (Eccl 2:1–8).

The economic system under the Persians was marked by mobility. There was ample opportunity to move up or down the economic ladder, often rapidly. Excessive debt was rampant. Many individuals were forced into debt just to feed their families, or forced to work extra to pay off their debt. We have evidence that the extremely rich were building their own prisons in order to hold those who could not pay their debt.[6] The Per-

---

5. Seow, *Ecclesiastes*, 21–23.
6. Seow, *Ecclesiastes*, 31.

sians also changed rules about land ownership so that it no longer passed from parent to child. Many land grants were distributed arbitrarily or at the whim of certain rulers or rich elites. In such an economic context, the words in Ecclesiastes become even more understandable. When economic security becomes tenuous because of the capricious environment, one can understand why the author would be so skeptical about the future. The book shows an epistemological uncertainty that parallels the relationship between Persian leadership and rapid economic change.

Ecclesiastes and Pope Francis

The way the tradition has cultivated Ecclesiastes and included it among Scripture provides a deep theological basis for the reflections of Pope Francis. When Francis says that "there is still an area of uncertainty" in the quest to seek God, one might initially recoil. How can the pope talk of uncertainty? We are inquisitive, prone to ask hard questions. When discussing preaching, Francis says that we must "keep in mind that we should never respond to questions that nobody asks."[7] In other words, we must engage the questions that naturally arise from the human situation. Ecclesiastes testifies to the fact that the church need not fear such hard questions, especially those that are grounded in the fundamental experience of being human. It is legitimate to question the benefits of righteousness in the face of unwarranted suffering. Such skepticism and hard questions come not only from the margins; Scripture places it on the lips of Solomon, someone at the very heart of the tradition. For Pope Francis, uncertainty seems to be necessary in order to leave room for God: "if one has the answers to all the questions—that is proof that God is not with him." Moreover, he claims, "uncertainty is in every true discernment that is open to finding confirmation in spiritual consolation."[8] Admitting, naming, discussing, questioning—these are the very things that, in Francis's vision, opens us up to God. The church need not fear them, nor should individuals.

The other connection between Ecclesiastes and Francis seems to be experience. One way of reading Ecclesiastes's words is that its author has let experience outweigh the party line. A close examination of injustice in the world led to hard questions. This, too, seems to be the fire in which Francis's spine was forged. His constant call to push the church to the

---

7. Francis, *Evangelii Gaudium*, 155.
8. Spadaro, "Interview with Pope Francis," para. 79.

margins of society leads to experiences that force hard questions with no easy answers. Theological reflection is contextual. Your context impacts how you view God. Francis, for instance, recommends that Christians should "live on the border and be audacious." He gives a concrete example, that we should not just go and observe a tough, drug-riddled neighborhood, but we should "live there and understand the problem from the inside." One must "experience poverty."[9]

Knowing and experiencing the world is dangerous, because you don't know where it will lead or the kinds of questions it will ask, much less the kinds of answers one might venture to give. Yet, this is where Francis seems to want to lead. Francis and the author of Ecclesiastes seem to agree that uncertainty is a necessary element of the faith journey, and we must embrace and admit that we don't have all the answers, even as we seek to continue to ask new questions.

Mark 9:2–8: The Transfiguration

If we turn to the New Testament, we find several texts that will continue this same theme—when dealing with faith and God, there must be an area of uncertainty. Francis repeatedly speaks of the importance of experience as foundational to a life of faith. Here we will look at the story of the transfiguration from the Gospel of Mark (9:2–8), which suggests that knowing God is experiential, not something that can be held in perpetuity.

The transfiguration of Jesus, in which Jesus is transformed before the eyes of three disciples (Peter, James, and John), is a high point in Mark's Gospel. It follows Jesus's first prediction of his death and resurrection, in which the disciples (particularly Peter) are unable to see things from God's point of view (8:27–33).

Jesus takes the three disciples up a mountain and his appearance becomes so garishly white that this could be an advertisement for Clorox. Moses and Elijah appear alongside Jesus and they talk amongst themselves. The imagery and motifs in this story fit into a familiar type of story that is called a "theophany," which means a transcendent experience through which humans experience the divine realm. In this particular story, the mountain, the bright whiteness, and the cloud are all common elements of theophanies in the Old Testament or other ancient literature.[10] These three disciples, then,

---

9. Spadaro, "Interview with Pope Francis," para. 99.
10. Marcus, *Mark 8–16*, 631–32. The story here shows similarities to the story of

are being given a unique experience, a glimpse at the divine reality that simmers below the surface of Jesus's earthly ministry.

The fascinating part of this story for our current purposes has to do with the response from Peter. He says, "Rabbi, it is good for us to be here! Let us make three tents, one for you, one for Moses, and one for Elijah" (9:5; author's translation). The next verse then provides more information, after the fact, of Peter's state of mind: "for he did not know how he should respond for they were exceedingly afraid" (9:6; author's translation). Peter is flummoxed and terrified, which, given what he had just seen, might be a legitimate reaction. After seeing this vision of Jesus's true identity, Peter's instinct is to create a shrine. The word for tent in verse 5 is the same word that the Jewish people used for the tabernacle, the tent in which Yahweh's presence dwelled in the Old Testament (e.g., Exod 27:21). Peter wants to take what he had just experienced and bottle it, so he can keep sipping from it for the rest of his life. He thought the journey was over and the place of arrival had been reached. Instead, a cloud envelops them, and the episode ends. Jesus does not even respond to Peter's suggestion; he just keeps moving. As they come back down from the mountain, Jesus readjusts their focus, back to the real endgame for his story, which is his own death and resurrection (Mark 9:9).

Peter's reaction to the theophany is to want to grasp it and hold it, to try to freeze a certain moment in time. He wants to domesticate, which is a ploy for certainty—to be able to hold on to something, know what it is, and have control over it.

We often want to have one moment in time where we suddenly say: "Aha! Here it is." Such an approach to God and religious experience is denigrated in many of Pope Francis's theological statements. For instance, he says that "finding God in all things is not an 'empirical *eureka*.'" *Eureka* is a Greek word from the scientific realm (legend attributes it to the ancient Greek scholar Archimedes). It simply means, "I have found it." We can imagine Peter on that mountain, amazed by the experience, shouting "Eureka! I've finally found it." His desire to hold on to it is understandable. But, according to Pope Francis, such a reaction is inappropriate: "When we desire to encounter God we would like to verify him immediately by an empirical method. But you cannot meet God this way." The "risk" in meeting God this way, says Francis, is that there is a "willingness to explain

---

Moses from Exodus 34:29.

too much" and to claim that "'God is here.'"[11] Our experience of God is through a journey, not the erection of a shrine. In his first homily after his election as Pope, Francis emphasized this very theme: "our life is a journey and when we stop, there is something wrong."[12] Francis points to Abraham as the perfect example. He left his home, not really knowing where he was going, and he, like many of the ancestors of our faith, "died seeing the good that was promised, but from a distance." So it was for Peter. At his best, he wants Jesus in a bottle; at his worst, he denies him. At the end of the Gospel of Mark (16:1–8), Peter does not make an appearance, but there is a promise that Jesus will meet him again in Galilee. Even in the light of the resurrection, the final image in the Gospel is one of a journey and a promise of little more than that the journey will continue. We must, Francis says, keep "going, walking, doing, searching, seeing . . . we must enter into the adventure of the quest for meeting God."[13]

Romans 9–11

Paul's letter to the church in Rome is his longest and most theologically sophisticated letter. Unlike most of his letters, which are written to communities he himself started, the gospel reached Rome without Paul. Paul wrote this letter from Corinth, sometime between the years 55 and 58 of the first century. One of the reasons Paul writes this letter is to curry support for his future plans to preach the gospel in Spain (see Rom 15:22–33), for which Rome would provide a convenient base of operations.

Ethnic Tensions within Early Roman Christianity

According to the Roman historian Suetonius, in 49 CE there was a riot within the Jewish community in Rome over someone named "Chrestus," which is probably a misunderstanding of "Christ." This is the earliest historical reference to Jesus outside of the New Testament. We conclude from this evidence that Christianity initially arrived and was cultivated in Rome within the Jewish community. At the same time, we have evidence of a significant influx of gentile—meaning, non-Jewish—Christians within

---

11. Spadaro, "Interview with Pope Francis," para. 80.
12. Palmo, "Francis' Agenda," para. 4.
13. Spadaro, "Interview with Pope Francis" para. 80.

the Roman church. Thus, we can reconstruct a basic dynamic of the early church in Rome: it was a blend of Jews and gentiles.

Paul writes six to eight years after the riot mentioned by Suetonius, but the ethnic tension in the Roman community is still palpable. In the opening chapters of the letter, Paul argues extensively that there is no advantage to being a Jew or a gentile, for all are equally under the power of sin (Rom 3:21–26). Justification before God, for Paul, is now to be based on faith, because God is a God of Jew and gentile alike (Rom 3:29).

In chapters 9–11 of Romans, Paul turns to a specific question related to the ethnic tension discussed here: why are so few of his fellow Jews coming to believe in Jesus as the Messiah, while the mission to the gentiles has been wildly successful? Paul addresses this question with some of his most theologically deft argumentation, which we will explore below. At the same time, despite his hard work and intricate ways of approaching the problem, he arrives at no definitive answers. In the end, he is left with questions and a considerable degree of uncertainty.

Analysis of Paul's Argument in Romans 9–11

In chapters 9–11 of his letter to the Romans, Paul turns full force to this question: If Israel is God's chosen people, why did God choose to include the gentiles, and why are many Jews not accepting Jesus? This is a deeply personal question for Paul, a Jew himself, who was responsible for the mission to the gentiles within the early church (see Gal 1–2). His personal turmoil is palpable from the outset: "I have great sorrow and unceasing anguish in my heart" (Rom 9:2). One can understand why. Paul, as a Jew who believes in Jesus, may have experienced painful estrangement from friends or family as a result of his belief in Jesus. We don't have direct evidence for this, but whether personal, or just at the level of his own ethnic identity and background, he has a strong personal involvement "for the sake of [his] own people" (9:3).

The argument that Paul presents is complicated and tangled up with intricate interpretations of the Old Testament. Looking at two aspects of these chapters—God's freedom and the mystery of God—will give us a sense of his overall argument. As we will see, Paul ends by describing a God whose ways are ultimately unknowable.

God's Freedom

In chapter 9, after stating the problem (of his fellow Jews who are not believing in Jesus) and noting his own emotional response (9:1–5), Paul spends most of the chapter building an argument about God. He turns to an example from the Old Testament: Jacob and Esau, the twin sons of Isaac and Rebecca. Paul notes that the Old Testament testifies that God chose to love one and to hate the other (Mal 1:2–3). This might seem unfair, like God is randomly playing favorites. For Paul, it is not unfair because God is able to do whatever God wants. To support such an idea, Paul quotes Exodus 33:19, in which God says to Moses: "I will have mercy on whom I have mercy, and I will have compassion on whom I have compassion" (Rom 9:15). He provides Pharaoh as another example, whose heart God hardens in the book of Exodus (Exod 4:21). Pharaoh was ready to let Moses's people go after the first plague, but God hardens Pharaoh's heart so that he would not let the people go, allowing God to send more plagues and show divine power.

In Romans 9:19–21, Paul provides a metaphor for the God he desires to depict: a potter shaping a lump of clay. Can a lump of clay give directions to the artist? Is it not up to the potter to decide whether the clay should become a chalice or an ashtray? This illustrates the point for Paul: "who, indeed, are you, a human being, to argue with God?" (9:20). When put so bluntly, it seems obvious that God can do whatever God wants.

There is, however, a deep theological problem here, which my students are usually quick to point out: "but that means we don't have free will!" Indeed, we like to think that we make choices that influence the outcome of our lives, particularly when our spiritual destiny is involved. Paul is suggesting the opposite: God can do whatever God wants irrespective of the individual will of humanity. Complaining about free will, though valid in a certain way, does not meet Paul's challenge directly. Paul intends to circumvent humanity altogether: "so it depends not on human will . . . but on God" (9:16). Beverly Roberts Gaventa summarizes Paul's perspective concisely: "If God chooses some and not others, that reflects only God's freedom and offers no basis for complaint."[14] Or, as I've heard her say more colloquially to her students (including me) on several occasions: "It's about God, stupid."

---

14. Gaventa, "Taken for Granted," 82–83.

Paul continues his argument in chapters 10 and 11 of Romans to try to build an argument why, ultimately, the destiny of the Jewish people is one of salvation. He uses the book of Hosea from the Old Testament to suggest that those people who were not God's people eventually will be. He asks, "has God rejected his people? By no means!" (Rom 11:1). While his arguments here may not always be completely coherent, Paul seems convinced that, somehow, God is working to achieve salvation for both Jew and gentile.

The Mystery of God in Romans 11:25-36

Paul's final reflection in Romans 11:33-36 moves in a completely different direction:

> O the depth of the riches and wisdom and knowledge of God! How unsearchable are his judgments and how inscrutable his ways!
> "For who has known the mind of the Lord?
> Or who has been his counselor?" (Rom 11:33-34)

It is still about God, but Paul has moved beyond what he knows God to have done, to the mystery of how or why God has done it. In the previous analysis of Paul's arguments, it is quite clear that Paul has thought a lot about this topic. He is not just randomly throwing words at the problem. He also is very personally and emotionally involved. Despite all of that thinking, working, and involvement, Paul essentially just throws up his hands in ignorance. His questions are not answered. In the end, God is a mystery. Who are we to think that we can know the mind of the Lord?

Paul's thoughts here are the result of a contradiction between theology and reality. Paul likely grew up with a specific ideology of God's election of Israel and the special covenant based on that election. But then his experience of the quick and successful inclusion of the gentiles into the plan of God causes him to reassess what he thought to be true. While questions here about free will are worth asking, Paul's argument is unabashedly theological; it's about God, stupid.

Paul is uncertain. His uncertainty is all the more remarkable when seen in the broader context of his letters, in which he usually is quite sure what he thinks about things. He is an apostle sent by God (a fact about which he often reminds his readers). He offers commands from Jesus (1 Cor 7:10) or directly from himself (1 Cor 7:12). When no command from the Lord is available to him, he claims that his opinion is trustworthy (1 Cor 7:25). Paul claims that his gospel is not from human origin. He received his gospel "through a revelation of Jesus Christ" (Gal 1:12). At times, even his travel plans are from divine revelation (Gal 2:1) or spiritual in nature (Rom 15:30–32; 1 Thess 2:18). Although he admits that the gospel does not make sense according to human wisdom (1 Cor 1:18–25) and that he does not present it with powerful eloquence (1 Cor 2:1–5), he nevertheless thinks he knows what the core of the gospel is (1 Cor 2:2–5; Gal 1:6–10). In light of all of this, Paul's lack of certainty at the end of Romans 9–11 stands out. He is certain of his reading of the landscape. He is convinced of simultaneously contradictory propositions: God chose Israel uniquely and has suddenly decided to include the gentiles. How this works out from God's point of view, he can't fully say. God is a mystery, which leads to Paul's uncertainty. Paul here demonstrates uncertainty in a life of faith, a willingness not to overexplain, to allow some questions to remain unanswered.

Conclusion

We have explored here three different parts of the Bible, one from the Old Testament and two from the New Testament, all with a remarkable openness to unanswered questions in a life of faith. Whether couched as epistemological skepticism (Ecclesiastes); reticence to codify and enshrine (the transfiguration); or openness to mystery and unanswered questions (Romans 9–11), all these texts suggest not only that we might experience unanswered questions, but more—that they should be expected and embraced.

We can tie such texts to foundational statements of Pope Francis. Many of the quotations I have supplied throughout this chapter come from the first extended interview with Francis, done by Antonio Spadaro. I would argue that the themes Francis emphasized early on are the same to which he turns again and again. If someone has all the answers, Francis says, that is "proof that God is not with him. It means that he is a false prophet using religion for himself." There must always be, Francis says, an "area of uncertainty" in our explorations of God. Total certainty is "not good."[15] The basis of such thoughts for Pope Francis is experience. Our ideas and knowledge about what is true should not always be didactic and doctrinal. Cardinal Blase Cupich, whom Francis appointed archbishop of Chicago in 2014, put a fine point on this when discussing Francis. He says that those

15. Spadaro, "Interview with Pope Francis," para. 79.

who criticize Pope Francis "because of his turn to real life experience fail to appreciate that he is calling people to a more authentic way of knowing and learning. He is challenging them about how they are informed . . . instead of approaching life from the thirty thousand foot level of ideas, he challenges us policy makers and elected officials—indeed all of us—to experience the life of everyday and real people."[16] Cupich goes on to quote Francis from *Evangelii Gaudium*, when he says: "reality is greater than ideas."

Many people today approach or define faith as believing a set of propositions, signing on the dotted line in assent to statements that are true. The biblical texts explored here testify to something different, that there is always an experiential side of faith, and that that experience does not translate well, or at all, to codification. Francis seems to share this conviction when he says that, "if the Christian is a restorationist, a legalist, if he wants everything clear and safe, then he will find nothing."[17] Past experience and tradition are not there simply to codify and explain, but should ultimately "open up new areas to God."[18] The pope does not eschew all doctrine, of course, but does reject a "doctrinal security" in favor of simply trusting God. This seems to be essentially what the apostle Paul is doing in Romans 9–11, trusting God because nothing seems to make sense based on what he thought he knew to be true.

Pope Francis turns to a biblical image for what God is like: the gentle breeze encountered by Elijah. In 1 Kings 19, God tells Elijah to stand on a mountain, for God is going to pass by. There was a great wind, an earthquake, and a fire, but God was not in any of these things. Then Elijah experiences God though something that is hard to translate. It was classically formulated as a "still small voice" in the King James Bible. More recent translations call it a "tiny whispering sound" (NAB) or a "sheer silence." We might connect this theologically with John 3:8, in which Jesus describes the Spirit to Nicodemus: "the wind blows where it wants and you hear its voice, but where it is from or where it is going you do not know" (author's translation). God is a breeze that blows; we can sense it, experience it, but it is ultimately mysterious, and leaves as many questions, if not more, than it answers. These more ephemeral ways of understanding a life of faith provide little to hang on to, but they speak powerfully to what it is often like to be a human seeking a life of faith. We

16. As quoted in Palmo, "For Chicago," para. 21.
17. Spadaro, "Interview with Pope Francis," para. 82.
18. Spadaro, "Interview with Pope Francis," para. 82.

encounter our lives, or even God, like *hevel*—a mist or a vapor—rather than something we can grasp. Allowing questions and uncertainty their due place might allow us to be open to God and to hold that love and relationship with an aroma.

Bibliography

Allen, John L. *The Francis Miracle: Inside the Transformation of the Pope and the Church.* New York: Time, 2015.
Anderson, Francis I., and David Noel Freedman. *Amos.* Anchor Yale Bible Series. New Haven, CT: Yale University Press, 1989.
Auguet, Roland. *Cruelty and Civilization: The Roman Games.* London: Allen & Unwin, 1972.
Bauckham, Richard. *The Bible and Ecology: Rediscovering the Community of Creation.* Waco, TX: Baylor University Press, 2010.
———. *Climax of Prophecy: Studies on the Book of Revelation.* Edinburgh: T. & T. Clark, 2000.
———. *Living with Other Creatures: Green Exegesis and Theology.* Waco, TX: Baylor University Press, 2011.
Benedict XVI. *Caritas in Veritate.* http://w2.vatican.va/content/benedict-xvi/en/encyclicals/documents/hf_ben-xvi_enc_20090629_caritas-in-veritate.html.
———. "General Audience, Wednesday, 26 August, 2009." http://w2.vatican.va/content/benedict-xvi/en/audiences/2009/documents/hf_ben-xvi_aud_20090826.html.
———. "Meeting of the Holy Father Benedict XVI with the Clergy of the Diocese of Bolzano-Bressanone." https://w2.vatican.va/content/benedict-xvi/en/speeches/2008/august/documents/hf_ben-xvi_spe_20080806_clero-bressanone.html.
Black, C. Clifton. *Mark.* Abingdon New Testament Commentaries. Nashville: Abingdon, 2011.
Blount, Brian K. *Revelation: A Commentary.* The New Testament Library. Louisville, KY: Westminster John Knox, 2009.
Bolen, Donald. "Mercy." In *A Pope Francis Lexicon*, edited by Joshua J. McElwee and Cindy Wooden, 126–34. Collegeville, MN: Liturgical, 2018.
Bond, Sarah. "The Ancient Crocodile Hunters that Helped to Supply the Roman Games." *Forbes*, June 12, 2017. http://www.forbes.com/sites/drsarahbond/2017/06/12/the-ancient-crocodile-hunters-that-helped-to-supply-the-roman-games/.
Carroll, Mark Daniel R. *Contexts for Amos: Prophetic Poetics in Latin American Perspective.* Sheffield, UK: Sheffield Academic, 1992.
The Catechism of the Catholic Church. http://www.vatican.va/archive/ENG0015/__P19.HTM.

BIBLIOGRAPHY

Cunningham, Philip. "Is the Pope 'Anti-Jewish'? No, but Here Is Why His Critics Think So." *Commonweal*, May 8, 2017. https://www.commonwealmagazine.org/pope-'anti-jewish'.

Davey, Sanjeev, and Anuradha Davey. "Assessment of Smartphone Addiction in Indian Adolescents." *International Journal of Preventive Medicine* 5 (2014) 1500–1511.

Dion, Paul E. "YHWH as Storm-God and Sun-God: The Double Legacy of Egypt and Canaan as Reflected in Psalm 104." *Zeitschrift für die Alttestamentliche Wissenschaft* 103 (2009) 43–71.

Downs, David J. *Alms: Charity, Reward, and Atonement in Early Christianity*. Waco, TX: Baylor University Press, 2016.

Ellis, Robert R. "Amos Economics." *Review and Expositor* 107 (2010) 463–79.

Epp, Eldon Jay. *Junia: The First Woman Apostle*. Minneapolis: Fortress, 2005.

Esteves, Junno Arocho. "Pontifical Commission for Latin America Proposes Synod on Women." *National Catholic Reporter*, April 11, 2018. https://www.ncronline.org/news/people/pontifical-commission-latin-america-proposes-synod-women.

Fiorenza, Elisabeth Schüssler. *Changing Horizons: Explorations in Feminist Interpretation*. Minneapolis: Fortress, 2013.

Flannery, Austin. *Vatican Council II: Volume 1 The Conciliar and Post Conciliar Documents*. Northport, NY: Costello, 1975.

Francis. *Amoris Laetitia*. https://w2.vatican.va/content/francesco/en/apost_exhortations/documents/papa-francesco_esortazione-ap_20160319_amoris-laetitia.html.

———. *Evangelii Gaudium*. https://w2.vatican.va/content/francesco/en/apost_exhortations/documents/papa-francesco_esortazione-ap_20131124_evangelii-gaudium.html.

———. *Gaudete et Exsultate*. http://w2.vatican.va/content/francesco/en/apost_exhortations/documents/papa-francesco_esortazione-ap_20180319_gaudete-et-exsultate.html.

———. "Homily of Holy Father Francis." http://w2.vatican.va/content/francesco/en/homilies/2013/documents/papa-francesco_20130708_omelia-lampedusa.html.

———. *Laudato Si'*. http://w2.vatican.va/content/francesco/en/encyclicals/documents/papa-francesco_20150524_enciclica-laudato-si.html.

———. *Misericordiae Vultus: Bull of Indiction of the Extraordinary Jubilee of Mercy*. https://w2.vatican.va/content/francesco/en/apost_letters/documents/papa-francesco_bolla_20150411_misericordiae-vultus.html.

———. *Morning Homilies in the Chapel of St. Martha's Guest House: March 22–July 26, 2013*. Translated by Dinah Livingstone. Maryknoll: Orbis, 2015.

———. *Morning Homilies II in the Chapel of St. Martha's Guest House: September 2, 2013–January 31, 2014*. Translated by Dinah Livingstone. Maryknoll: Orbis, 2016.

———. *Morning Homilies III in the Chapel of St. Martha's Guest House: February 3–June 30, 2014*. Translated by Dinah Livingstone. Maryknoll: Orbis, 2016.

Frankel, Todd C. "The Cobalt Pipeline: Tracing the Path from Deadly Hand-Dug Mines in Congo to Consumers' Phones and Laptops." *Washington Post*, September 30, 2016. https://www.washingtonpost.com/graphics/business/batteries/congo-cobalt-mining-for-lithium-ion-battery/?hpid=hp_hp-top-table-main_cobaltflipper-916a%3Ahomepage%2Fstory.

Gaillardetz, Richard R. "Infallibility and the Ordination of Women." *Louvain Studies* 21 (1996) 3–24.

BIBLIOGRAPHY

Gajiwala, Astrid Lobo. "Women." In *A Pope Francis Lexicon*, edited by Joshua J. McElwee and Cindy Wooden, 190–95. Collegeville: Liturgical, 2018.

Gaventa, Beverly Roberts. "The God Who Will Not Be Taken for Granted: Reflections on Paul's Letter to the Romans." In *The Ending of Mark and the Ends of God: Essays in Memory of Donal Harrisville Juel*, edited by Patrick D. Miller and Beverly Roberts Gaventa, 77–89. Louisville, KY: Westminster John Knox, 2005.

Gilhus, Ingvild Saelid. *Animals, Gods, and Humans: Changing Attitudes to Animals in Greek, Roman, and Early Christian Thought*. London: Routledge, 2006.

Glatz, Carol. "Devil Prefers Comfy, Business-Savvy Church that Overlooks Truth, Pope Says." *Catholic News Service*, May 23, 2017. https://cnstopstories.com/2017/05/23/devil-prefers-comfy-business-savvy-church-that-overlooks-truth-pope-says/.

———. "Pope Francis: Pray that Priests Never Use Law to Shut Door to Salvation." *America Magazine*, October 19, 2017. https://www.americamagazine.org/faith/2017/10/19/pope-francis-pray-priests-never-use-law-shut-door-salvation.

Gray, Mark M. "Proud to be Catholic? A Groundbreaking America Survey Asks Women about Their Lives in the Church." *America Magazine*, January 16, 2018. https://www.americamagazine.org/faith/2018/01/16/proud-be-catholic-groundbreaking-america-survey-asks-women-about-their-lives.

Green, Joel B. *The Gospel of Luke*. New International Commentary on the New Testament. Grand Rapids, MI: Eerdmans, 1997.

Habel, Norman C. "Earth First: Inverse Cosmology in Job." In *The Earth Story in Wisdom Traditions*, edited by Norman C. Habel and Shirley Wurst, 65–77. Sheffield, UK: Sheffield Academic, 2001.

Hall, Douglas J. *Imaging God: Dominion as Stewardship*. Eugene, OR: Wipf & Stock, 2004.

Hays, Richard B. *Echoes of Scripture in the Gospels*. Waco, TX: Baylor University Press, 2016.

Hillel, Daniel. *The Natural History of the Bible: An Environmental Exploration of the Hebrew Scriptures*. New York: Columbia University Press, 2006.

Hillis, Gregory K. "'Filled with Words of Love': Pope Francis on Dialogue as Spiritual Conversion." *ABC Religion & Ethics*, March 16, 2016. http://www.abc.net.au/religion/articles/2016/03/16/4426057.htm.

Horrell, David G. *The Bible and the Environment: Towards a Critical Ecological Biblical Theology*. London: Equinox, 2010.

Hudock, Barry. "When My Daughter Whispered to Me, 'I Wish Girls Could be Priests,' I Didn't Know What to Say." *America*, March 8, 2018. https://www.americamagazine.org/faith/2018/03/08/when-my-daughter-whispered-me-i-wish-girls-could-be-priests-i-didnt-know-what-say.

Hughes, Donald J. *Environmental Problems of the Greeks and Romans: Ecology in the Ancient Mediterranean*. Baltimore: Johns Hopkins University Press, 2014.

Hunwicke, John. "Peter Says No." *First Things*, February 7, 2017. https://www.firstthings.com/web-exclusives/2017/02/peter-says-no.

Ivereigh, Austen. *The Great Reformer: Francis and the Making of a Radical Pope*. New York: Picador, 2014.

John Paul II. *Ordinatio Sacerdotalis: On Reserving Priestly Ordination to Men Alone*. https://w2.vatican.va/content/john-paul-ii/en/apost_letters/1994/documents/hf_jp-ii_apl_19940522_ordinatio-sacerdotalis.html.

Jones, James. *Jesus and the Earth*. London: SPCK, 2003.

BIBLIOGRAPHY

Josephus. *Antiquities.* Translated by Ralph Marcus. Loeb Classical Library. Cambridge, MA: Harvard University Press, 1943.

Juel, Donald H. *A Master of Surprise: Mark Interpreted.* Minneapolis: Augsburg Fortress, 2002.

Just, Arthur, ed. *Ancient Christian Commentary on Scripture: New Testament III, Luke.* Downers Grove, IL: InterVarsity Press Academic, 2003.

Kahan, Dan M., et al. "The Polarizing Impact of Science Literacy and Numeracy on Perceived Climate Change Risks." *Nature Climate Change* 2 (2013) 732–35.

Levine, Amy-Jill. *Short Stories by Jesus: The Enigmatic Parables of a Controversial Rabbi.* New York: HarperOne, 2015.

Limburg, James. "What Does It Mean to 'Have Dominion over the Earth?'" *Dialog* 10 (1971) 221–23.

Marcus, Joel. *Mark 8–16.* Anchor Yale Bible Series. New Haven: Yale University Press, 2009.

McDonagh, Sean. *The Greening of the Church.* Maryknoll, NY: Orbis, 1990.

Mickens, Robert. "Don't Say 'We Have Always Done Things This Way.'" *Commonweal*, May 1, 2017. https://www.commonwealmagazine.org/letter-rome-122.

Milanovic, Branko. *Global Inequality: A New Approach for the Age of Globalization.* Cambridge, MA: Belknap, 2016.

Murphy, Frederick J. *Religious World of Jesus.* Nashville: Abingdon, 1991.

Myers, Ched. *Binding the Strong Man: A Political Reading of Mark's Story of Jesus.* Maryknoll, NY: Orbis, 1988.

Naess, Arne. "The Basics of Deep Ecology." *Trumpeter* 21 (2005) 61–71.

Neruda, Pablo. *100 Love Sonnets: Cien Sonetos de Amor.* Translated by Stephen Tapscott. Austin: University of Texas Press, 1986.

O'Loughlin, Michael J. *The Tweetable Pope: A Spiritual Revolution in 140 Characters.* New York: HarperOne, 2015.

Palmieri-Billig, Lisa. "Italy's Rabbis Protest—Controversy over Title and Program of Italian Biblical Association Colloquium." *Vatican Insider*, March 20, 2017. https://www.lastampa.it/2017/03/20/vaticaninsider/italys-rabbis-protest-controversy-over-title-and-program-of-italian-biblical-association-colloquium-kiRSt87krpVb6CjEtUoAsJ/pagina.html.

Palmo, Rocco. "For Chicago, the 'Thunder' Is In—Cupich Named Corporation Sole." *Whispers in the Loggia* (blog), September 20, 2014. http://whispersintheloggia.blogspot.com/2014/09/for-chicago-thunder-is-in.html.

———. "Francis' Agenda: 'To Walk, To Build, to Profess Christ Crucified.'" *Whispers in the Loggia* (blog), March 14, 2013. http://whispersintheloggia.blogspot.com/2013/03/francis-agenda-to-walk-to-build-to.html.

Paul VI. "Dei Verbum." http://www.vatican.va/archive/hist_councils/ii_vatican_council/documents/vat-ii_const_19651118_dei-verbum_en.html.

———. *Inter Insigniores: On the Question of Admission of Women to the Ministerial Priesthood.* http://www.vatican.va/roman_curia/congregations/cfaith/documents/rc_con_cfaith_doc_19761015_inter-insigniores_en.html.

Pippin, Tina. *Death and Desire: The Rhetoric of Gender in the Apocalypse of John.* Louisville, KY: Westminster John Knox, 1992.

Plutarch. *Plutarch's Lives V: Agesilaus and Pompey; Pelopidas and Marcellus.* Translated by Bernadotte Perrin. Loeb Classical Library. Cambridge, MA: Harvard University Press, 1917.

BIBLIOGRAPHY

Pongratz-Lippitt, Christa. "Pope Francis Discusses Married Priests, Women Deacons with German Newspaper." *National Catholic Reporter*, March 10, 2017. https://www.ncronline.org/news/vatican/pope-francis-discusses-married-priests-women-deacons-german-newspaper.

"Pope at Santa Marta: 'There are Pharisees in the Church Today Like in the Time of Jesus.'" *Rome Reports*, October 19, 2017.. https://www.romereports.com/en/2017/10/19/pope-at-santa-marta-there-are-pharisees-in-the-church-today-like-in-the-time-of-jesus/.

Pope Francis Speaks to the United States and Canada: Speeches, Homilies, and Interviews. Huntington: Our Sunday Visitor, 2015.

"Pope: 'Where There Is No Mercy There Is No Justice.'" *Archdiocese of Malta*, March 24, 2015. http://thechurchinmalta.org/en/posts/47974/untitled-article.

Rossing, Barbara R. *The Choice Between Two Cities: Whore, Bride, and Empire in the Apocalypse.* Harrisburg, PA: Trinity, 1999.

Roukema, Riemer. "The Good Samaritan in Ancient Christianity." *Vigiliae Christianae* 58 (2004) 56–74.

Saldarini, Anthony J. *Pharisees, Scribes and Sadducees in Palestinian Society.* Grand Rapids, MI: Eerdmans, 2001.

Seow, C. L. *Ecclesiastes.* Anchor Yale Bible Series. New York: Doubleday, 1997.

Shannon, William H., and Christine M. Bochen, eds. *Thomas Merton: A Life in Letters, the Essential Collection.* Notre Dame: Ave Maria, 2010.

Shelton, Jo-Ann. *As the Romans Did: A Source Book in Roman Social History.* New York: Oxford University Press, 1988.

Spadaro, Antonio. "Interview with Pope Francis." http://w2.vatican.va/content/francesco/en/speeches/2013/september/documents/papa-francesco_20130921_intervista-spadaro.html.

Squires, Nick. "Benedict XVI—The 'Green' Pope." *The Telegraph*, June 21, 2011. http://www.telegraph.co.uk/news/worldnews/the-pope/8589031/Benedict-XVI-The-green-Pope.html.

Tossell, Chad, et al. "Exploring Smartphone Addiction: Insights from Long-Term Telemetric Behavioral Measures." *International Journal of Interactive Mobile Technologies* 9 (2015) 37–43.

White, Lynn. "The Historical Roots of our Ecologic Crisis." *Science* 155 (1967) 1203–7.

Wooden, Cindy. "Do Not Be Fooled by 'Doctors of the Law' Who Limit God's Love, Says Pope Francis." *Catholic Herald*, October 15, 2015. http://www.catholicherald.co.uk/news/2015/10/15/do-not-be-fooled-by-doctors-of-law-who-limit-gods-love-says-pope-francis/.

Wooden, Cindy, and Joshua J. McElwee, eds. *A Pope Francis Lexicon.* Collegeville, MN: Liturgical, 2018.

Wright, John R. "Patristic Testimony on Women's Ordination in Inter Insigniores." *Theological Studies* 58 (1997) 516–26.

Scripture Index

Old Testament

Genesis

1	54
1:26–28	43
1:26	4, 5, 44
1:28	44
3:14–19	58

Exodus

4:21	124
27:21	121
34:29	120n10

Leviticus

19:18	87

Deuteronomy

5:9–10	83
20:14	14
25:19	14
28:1–2	117
28:15	117

1 Samuel

13	13
14:24–46	13
15	13, 15
15:3	14, 15
15:9	13
15:10	13
15:22	14

1 Kings

19	8, 127

Job

4:7–8	49
6:1–13	48
8:1–10	49
9:8–10	49
9:22	49
10:3–6	48
12:7–9	49
12:29	51
15:18–20	49
38–39	50
38:4	50
38:19	50
38:22	50
38:35	50
39:1	50

Job (continued)

39:9	50
39:18	51
39:26	50

Psalms

8:5	44
6:6–8	45
24:1	47
37:11	8
72:8	46
72:12–14	46
82:1	5
103:3–4	93
104	52
104:1–9	53
104:10–30	53
104:14–15	53
104:24	54
104:27–30	54
146:7–9	94
148	54
148:11–12	55

Proverbs

1:33	117

Ecclesiastes

1:1–11	118
1:2	116
1:4–11	116
1:5	116
1:6	116
1:7	116
1:8	116
2:1–8	118
8:14–15	116
9:2	118
9:11–12	117

Isaiah

5:8	27
11:6–7	58, 59
41	57

Ezekiel

34:2–4	46n12

Jonah

1:2	19
3:10	19
4:2	19, 82
4:10–11	20

Hosea

6	109
6:6	102

Amos

2:6–7	27
5:11	28
5:18–20	29
5:21–23	29
5:24	29
6:1	28
6:4–7	28
7	97
7:9	97
8:3	98
8:5	97
8:9–10	98
8:11–12	98

Micah

1:1	99
2:1–2	27
3:1–3	99
3:11	99

SCRIPTURE INDEX

6:6–8	100

Malachi

1:2–3	124

Deuterocanonical

Tobit

3:2	84
4:5–11	84
12:8–9	84

Sirach

2:8	118
3:30	85
17:22	85
29:12	85
40:24	85

Pseudepigrapha

1 Enoch

26:6	58

New Testament

Matthew

1:1–17	9
5:1–9	31
5:3	8
5:21–22	101
9	109
9:9–13	102
9:16–17	102
12	109
12:3–8	103
12:11–12	103
18	92
18:32–33	93

23	105, 109
23:3	109
23:6–7	109
23:8–10	110
23:13–26	32n17
23:16–17	109
23:23	109
23:24	109

Mark

1:10	57
1:12–13	60
1:13	57, 58, 59, 61
2	14
2:18–22	15
2:22	16
4–5	18, 19
4:1–20	16
4:13	16
4:19	18
4:26–29	16
4:27	16
4:30–32	16
4:40	17
4:41	17
5	17
5:7	17
5:15	17
7:5	108
8:27–33	120
9:2–8	120
9:5	121
9:6	121
9:9	121
10:45	62
12:13	41
16:1–8	122

Luke

1:1–4	31
1:50	91
1:52–53	30
1:72	91
1:78	91

SCRIPTURE INDEX

Luke (continued)

6	33
6:17–21	31
6:24–25	31
6:20	8
7:30	87
8:18–30	24
9:54–56	89
10:25–37	86
10:28	87
10:33	90
11:29–30	82
11:37–54	82
15:11–32	91
15:32	91
16:13	33
16:15	87
16:19–31	30
16:29	31
18:18–25	91
18:23	91

John

1:43–51	71
2	75
3:8	127
4	89
8	9, 110

Acts

8:26–40	95
8:26	95
8:30	95
18:18	74

Romans

3:21–26	123
3:29	123
9–11	115, 122, 123, 126
9:1–5	124
9:2	123
9:3	123
9:15	124
9:16	124
9:19–21	124
11:25–36	125
11:33–34	125
15:22–33	122
15:30	126
16:1–2	72, 74, 75
16:4	74
16:6, 9, 12	74
16:7	72, 78, 79

1 Corinthians

1:10–17	72
1:18–25	126
2:2–5	126
3:5	75
4:9	72
7:10	125
7:12	125
7:25	126
14:32–36	74
15	71

2 Corinthians

3:5–6	75

Galatians

1–2	123
1:6–10	126
1:12	126
2:1	126
3:28	70, 72, 73

Ephesians

6:21	75

Philippians

1:1	76
3:4–6	108

Colossians

4:7	75

1 Thessalonians

1:1	72
2:6	72
2:18	126

1 Timothy

3:8–13	76
3:11	76

Hebrews

6:19	104

James

2:13	86

Revelation

2:13	35
2:14	35
2:19–23	36
2:20	35
3:17	35
3:19	35
11:15	34
12	35
12:9	36
13	35, 38
13:1	35
13:11	35
13:16–17	36
17:1–18	36
18	38
18:4	37
18:11–17	37
21	38
22	38
22:17	38